It's more than se

Suzie Hayman

It's more than sex!

A survival guide to the teenage years

Wildwood House

First published in Great Britain in 1986
by Wildwood House Ltd
Gower House,
Croft Road,
Aldershot,
Hants GU11 3HR

Hayman, Suzie
  It's more than sex.
  1. Adolescent psychology
  I. Title
  158'.1'088055   BF724

  ISBN 0-7045-0512-6

Printed and bound in Great Britain by
Biddles Ltd, Guildford and King's Lynn

This book is for the many young people who helped me, with their questions and comments – Jane, Steve, Hilary, Chrissy and all the others. Especial thanks are due to Alex, Tania, Marian, Hazel, Elaine, Christine and Stephen.

And to Vic, without whom no i would have been dotted, no t crossed and an awful lot of stones left unturned. Lucky thirteen, hokay, uh-huh?

Contents

Section 6. The Outside World

Introduction

Some adults are fond of saying your schooldays are 'the happiest days of your life'. Teenagers know better! The teenage years – or 'adolescence' – are as full of confusion and unhappiness as they are of excitement and fun. Adolescence is the time when your body and your emotions grow from child into adult. It doesn't happen overnight, and the journey can be a hard one. All teenagers worry during these years. Is my body normal? Are my feelings natural? Whether you are male or female, you will have these and many other questions, and will be as curious about the bodies and feelings of the other sex as you are about your own.

This book is written for both boys and girls, to answer as many of these questions as possible. The physical changes that happen during adolescence will be described fully for both. I hope that this may calm any fears you have about yourself, and satisfy the natural curiosity you also have about the opposite sex. Feelings about these changes, getting on with parents and other adults, getting on with friends, learning how to cope in the outside world – all these apply equally to both sexes.

You might also like your parents to leaf through these pages. They, too, went through everything you are experiencing. You may find this difficult to believe, and they may have forgotten, but it's true! If you have a hard time learning to stand on your own two feet, parents have as difficult a task. They must learn to let you go and to let you make your own mistakes without their protection. This book may help both teenagers and parents to understand each others' problems, and make getting on easier.

You may think that the point of growing up is that it gives you freedom. You can wear the clothes you like, come and go as you please and have the friends you choose. You'd be wrong. Very few adults are 'free' in this sense. Adults have more responsibilities than they have freedom. Just look at your parents and you'll see that this is true. But, what they often *do* have, is a certain measure of *control* – control over their lives and bodies, their beliefs and opinions. Adolescence is the time when you gradually learn to shift from having your parents and teachers look after you, be responsible for you, tell you what is right and what to think – in other words, *control* you – to doing it yourself. Many people drift through life letting things happen to them rather than making the best of opportunities. The more you learn about yourself and the world around you, the more you can decide what will happen in your life. People may have told you 'a little learning is a dangerous thing'. They're right – but not in the way they usually mean. The man who wrote this (Alexander Pope) actually meant that knowing *only* a little was bad, but knowing *plenty* was good!

However kind and helpful your parents will be, there are some questions you would rather not ask them. This is no insult to them, but a part of growing up. If this book does not have the answers, it should point you in the right direction. You can use the book in three ways:

You might like to start at the beginning and read straight through;

You might like to 'dip in' and just read certain chapters now, and keep the others for another time; or

You might have a particular question you want answering. In which case, you can use the Index to spot the subject.

You are a unique person. But what is happening to you now *has* happened to others before, however new and private it may seem to you. And, as difficult as it may seem, you *will* survive adolescence. I hope that this book helps you to do it in style!

1. In The Beginning – Puberty

'I couldn't understand what was happening to me. It seemed that one day I was a normal person and the next, I was this alien being – all hairy and sweaty and fat' – Jane R.

During your childhood, a hidden clock in your body ticks away and, at the right moment, it sets off a time bomb. We call it 'puberty', and this process changes your body from a child's into an adult's. For girls, the most noticeable event of puberty is the start of periods. Having a first 'wet dream' can be a similar milestone for boys. It certainly gives them as much of a shock! But puberty is not a single event. It takes several years and will affect both your body and your mind in many ways.

The first stage will start gradually. Girls usually notice this when they are 10 or 11, but for some it is as early as 9 or as late as 13 or 14. Boys are usually about a year later. In both sexes, the fine downy hair which covers the body will become coarser and darker in certain places. You will find that it becomes noticeable under your arms, on your legs, and, most especially, on your genitals – your 'private parts' – between your legs. Some boys find that hair grows on the chest – and so do some girls! The fine down between the breasts can become darker, and most women have a ring of long, fine hairs around the nipples.

Both boys and girls will put on weight. This is the time when mums, aunts and neighbours cluck sympathetically and mutter 'Puppy fat – you'll grow out of it!' You may find their attention embarrassing, but listen to them, because they are right. There is absolutely no need to panic and diet. In fact, going on a crash diet at this stage could even harm you. If you are a girl, a diet could make your periods stop, or delay them starting. This little bit of fat is natural and happens to everyone. It's a preparation

PUBERTY ~ countdown from birth at zero years
activate ~ glands, hair-growth, genital enlargement, breast growth.

for you becoming a woman and eventually, perhaps, a mother. Women have more 'subcutaneous' fat – that is, fat under the skin – to serve as a storehouse of energy and food for themselves and the baby when they become pregnant.

Girls will find that their hips get broader and that thighs and buttocks become fatter. Even your face may fill out. Most important of all, your breasts, which up to now had been flat with tiny pink nipples, will begin to swell. The skin around the nipples will start to bulge out and darken very slightly in colour. So will the skin around your genitals, and this too will become padded with fat. All women have three openings between their legs: the back passage, to pass solid waste; the vagina or sex passage, through which blood passes during a period; and the front passage or urethra, to pass water. As puberty goes on, the folds of skin and flesh at either side of your sex and water passages will also fill out and grow in size. These are called 'labia'. You might hear some people call this part of a woman's body her 'cunt', 'pussy' or 'fanny'. Men have two passages. The back passage is for solid waste. The front passage passes down the centre of the penis and carries waste water or urine and also the man's sex fluid – his semen or 'spunk'.

Just as noses and faces are different in everyone, so is the appearance of our genitals. In some women, the lips at either side of the two front openings are thick and wrinkled and hang down. In others, they are smaller and almost hidden in the hair that covers this part of your body, called 'pubic' hair. Don't be frightened and think that there is anything wrong with you if you are one of the people with large 'lips'. And don't think that these changes, which happen to *everyone*, are because of something you have done – such as rubbing these parts for the pleasant feelings it causes. This is called 'masturbation', and we'll talk about it later in the book. Most people do it at some point in their lives. It *can't* harm you or alter your body in any way!

Breasts also come in all different shapes and sizes. They can be apple-, pear- or cone- shaped. They can be large and soft, or small and hard. They can be mere pimples on a flat chest. Whichever, they are *normal* and you can't change them by rubbing with creams or doing excercises. They will temporarily grow in size if you get pregnant, go on the Pill, or make love! Apart from that, if you aren't happy, you have two choices: plastic surgery or changing your mind about them! Changing your mind is a lot cheaper.!

Boys will put on weight around their shoulders. Instead of that layer of fat, they put on muscle. As many as a third to a half of all boys will also find *their* breasts grow. This is quite normal – it's called 'gynaecomastia'. Unless you are very overweight, the pads of fat that give a girlish outline will disappear after 12 to 18 months, or sooner. As well as finding hair on the sexual organs, boys will also find it grows on the upper lips. Your penis will darken slightly in colour and grow. So will the testicles or 'balls'. These hang below the penis and contain a man's 'seed' or sperm. The bag they are in – the 'scrotum' – becomes wrinkled and covered in sparse, curly hair.

Men's sexual parts are also different shapes and sizes – all normal. Some men have a short penis some have a long, thin one. When a boy becomes sexually excited, his penis – also known as his 'cock', 'dick', 'prick' or 'willie' – will stiffen, swell and stand out from his body. This called having an 'erection'. It is also known as having a 'hard on' or 'the horn'. The size of your penis when it is limp or 'flaccid' is not neccessarily a clue to the size it will be when erect. A long, thin one will usually increase the width but not in length, while a short, fat one will swell lenthways. Most are roughly the same size when erect – so comparisons in the showers are unfair! The size of your penis proves nothing about your ability as a lover or a potential father. The quality of your lovemaking will be far more important than size to a partner. Comparisons can also give you the wrong idea about yourself. An object will always look shorter

from above than from the side. So, unless you line up in front of a mirror, other boys' penises will always look bigger to you than your own. The shaft of your penis will be the same colour as the skin on your body, except around its head or 'glans'. This will probably be a deeper pink or red colour. During an erection, it will flush a darker red or purple. You will also have veins running down the sides of the shaft which will swell and stand out when you become sexually excited. Most penises have a slight bend to either right or left – this is perfectly normal and nothing to worry about.

When it is limp, the end of the penis is covered with a hood of skin, called a foreskin. Sometimes this is trimmed back in an operation called 'circumcision'. The operation may be done for religious reasons or for medical ones, if the foreskin was too tight for it to be properly drawn back. Circumcised penises are often called 'roundheads' and uncircumcised 'cavaliers'. The names recall the English Civil War soldiers, who either had plain helmets or hats with feathers and frills. A circumcised penis may seem larger than an untouched one, although it isn't. This is just because, with the shiny glans showing, the organ looks as if it is about to swell up and become erect. Being circumcised or not will make no difference to your sexual feelings or abilities.

There are other changes that can cause you a lot of heartache. You can shoot up in height, gaining as much as 2 inches in as many months. It's as if you were to find yourself in another person's body overnight. It is hardly surprising that you trip over your own feet or knock things around. Lots of teenagers get into the habit of hunching over to try and hide their new bodies. This new body seems so odd to you that you imagine everyone is looking at you when you cross a room or walk down the street, when, in fact, they are not. You can't win – parents will tell you to straighten up and then tell you off for falling over something! Teenage clumsiness is not a sign of stupidity or laziness. It's your body and brain trying to readjust to the sudden differences. Last week when you reached for a cup, your arm was shorter. When you took a step, so were your legs. You can't be blamed for being slow to remember to reach a bit less. Adults forget about what happened to them when they were your age, and can be impatient with you at this time – remind them!

Your skin becomes coarser at this time, and minute glands start to produce more oil. This is called 'sebum'. It often blocks the pores – the tiny openings in your skin. This leads to black-heads, whiteheads and that most agonizing part of being a teenager – SPOTS!

Spots are not actually *caused* by a bad diet or sexy dreams or anything else. They are a fact of teenage life and only 1 in 10 of you won't suffer from them. All you can do is to make them as bearable as possible. If you eat lots of fried food, never get out of the house, stay up late every night and only wash once a week, you can't give yourself spots, but you won't be helping! The following tips aren't likely to actually clear spots or 'acne', but they will help to give your skin a healthy, glowing look that will make spots appear a lot less ghastly and also help to clear them up quickly. So, try to:

1) Eat plenty of fresh fruit and vegetables. Limit the chips, crisps, chocolates and fizzy drinks to an occasional treat

2) Get plenty of fresh air and exercise

3) Wash your face twice a day – too much washing and rubbing actually encourages the skin to be oily

4) Keep late nights for special occasions. The odd late night does no harm – but you do need plenty of sleep during these years

5) Avoid cover-up creams or make-up. They can encourage spots by stopping them clearing themselves. Don't use make up every day, and always remove it thoroughly at bedtime.

If your spots are really worrying you, go and see your doctor. There are ways of controlling acne and your doctor may agree that you need help. He or she can give you special strong creams or a course of antibiotics to clear up your skin.

You will also find that you sweat more now than you did as a child. Your feet, under your arms and around your genital organs will be particularly likely to get hot and damp. Sweat itself does not smell unpleasant. But stale sweat is like garden compost – it's a perfect growing medium for bacteria, which are tiny germs. These *do* smell, so you will find it a good idea to have a bath or shower every day, or, at least, to wash these parts thoroughly. Clean pants and socks daily and frequent changes of shirts or anything else worn next to the skin will make you a pleasant person to be near! Start using the family deodorant under your arms, too. Deodorants help to control your sweating, but you will find it a normal part of your life to get wet at times. Never, ever, use deodorants on your genital organs. This would make the delicate skin sting and could lead you to get an infection there. You don't need them anyway. The faint, fresh smell of human sweat is not really unpleasant; it is only nasty if left overnight. And the special scent given off by your sexual parts is actually sexy to a member of the opposite sex!

As you grow, you will find your voice changes, becoming deeper and more grown-up. Boys find this change dramatic, with a period during which the voice shoots up and down from a squeak to a boom. Very embarrassing!

There are other changes going on in your body – changes you cannot see. At the base of your brain, a tiny gland sends out special chemicals which are called hormones. These are messengers, and they tell bits of your body to act in various ways at certain times. They tell your body when to start growing hair, and when to make you taller. In girls, they tell the body when to start having periods. Hormones also make you feel emotions. A change in hormones can make you feel suddenly sad, angry, happy or tired, so teenagers can swing between all these moods without realizing why. There may seem to be no reason for a sudden depression – but it's probably your hormones having a practice!

Lots of teenagers are caught by surprise at the way their body alters at this time in their lives. As far back as you can remember, your body has been a certain shape. Suddenly, bits start sprouting and thickening and doing all sorts of weird things. It can be very easy to feel that something is out of step. You can be afraid that the new, and somewhat untidy, appearance of your genitals is 'wrong'. You can convince yourself it means you are deformed. But this won't be true. A *child's* body is smooth and neat. Adults are meant to be a bit rough around the edges! *Whatever* the size and shape of your body, it will be natural and normal and nothing to worry about.

2. Periods And Wet Dreams

'I don't remember whether my Mum had said anything about periods. It didn't sink in if she did, because my first one was a horrible shock. I found blood on my pants and was terrified. I burst into tears at school and a teacher took me home. I thought I was being punished for something' – Mandy J.

'My first wet dream happened when I was 13. I'll never forget how scared I was when I woke up. I didn't know what had happened and what the white stuff I found on my pyjamas was' – Mark M.

Periods and wet dreams are a landmark during puberty and they generally start some one to two years after your body has begun to turn from a child's into an adult's. Most girls have their first period around the age of 11 or 12. You may feel out of sorts for a few days and find yourself snapping at people for no reason. You may feel a slight cramp deep in your lower belly. But, for many, the first sign is a spot of blood on your pants. This might be a bright red or a brownish colour. We tend to think of blood as only showing if we've been cut or grazed. *This* blood is not from a wound, so you shouldn't be afraid that anything is wrong.

So why does it happen? The hormones we mentioned before tell your body to gain weight and height. They also tell certain organs inside you to start working. Your heart, liver, lungs and other organs have been working away since before you were born. But your ovaries and womb have been waiting for this signal and only now swing into use.

Your womb or uterus is about the size and shape of a pear. It hangs upside-down in your lower belly. Clench your fist and push it against your stomach below the navel – that's where your womb is, but 4-6 inches back. The womb is a very flexible

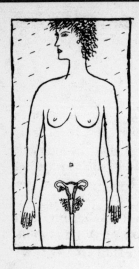

bag. If you do become pregnant, it will stretch to hold both the baby and the fluid it swims in. For now, it just waits and prepares. Each month, the lining of the womb builds up and waits for the arrival of a 'fertilized' egg: that is, an egg from your body that has met and joined up with sperm from a man. We'll discuss how this can happen in a later chapter! If such an egg does not arrive on cue, the lining will begin to come away. It is made of blood and some tissue, but is mainly water. You would actually lose about half a cupful of blood. This all seeps out of the middle opening between your legs – the vagina. This is a 'period' or 'menstruation'. Because it can be messy and uncomfortable, and most girls find it gives them cramps, we also call it 'the curse'. Because we are made to feel embarrassed, we may talk about 'Aunty coming for a call', or 'monthlies' or 'that time of the month' rather than say outright 'I've got my period' – especially in front of boys. This is a pity. 52% of the world has periods – why should you be ashamed of a perfectly natural, normal event? It's also a pity that boys are kept in the dark. When they don't know about periods, life can be uncomfortable for you both. Boys may embarrass you by trying to find out what's going on – the more it's kept a secret, the more they try to crack the code. They may also feel so fed up at being left out that they make nasty jokes and try to upset you. When they do know as much as you, however, it can make life very easy. Once boys understand you feel tense or are in pain at certain times and can't help it, they may be more helpful and sympathetic.

But where does the egg come from? There are two tubes that lead out of the top of your womb. These are called Fallopian tubes. At each end hangs an ovary. Ovaries are egg cases. They are each about the size and shape of a plum. An ovary contains about 30,000 minute bundles of cells, each of which could grow into a tiny egg. In fact, only about 400 are likely to mature in your lifetime. As the lining of your womb builds up, your hormones signal to an ovary. It spurts out an egg which travels down one of the tubes to your womb. This tiny egg, too small for the eye to see, will be washed away in the normal flow fluid from your womb and vagina.

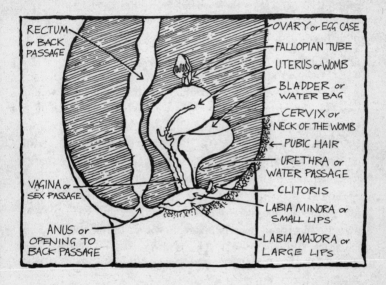

Your periods will probably settle down to arriving every 26-30 days and lasting for 4 to 5 days. In the first year or so, however, they may be shorter or longer and arrive at odd times. 'Ovulation' – which is when the egg is released – always comes 14 days *before* the period starts. You can sometimes tell when you ovulate. You may feel cramps or pains on one side of your lower belly. And you may find a thick, creamy white liquid on your pants. This discharge is another sign of your growing up. It is perfectly normal for your vagina or sex passage to be sticky. The skin on the walls and outside this passage is delicate and needs to be kept moist for it to stay healthy. A white or clear fluid oozes from the walls all the time. It can then seep out and is likely to be found on your pants. It becomes yellow/cream when it dries and may have a musky and not unpleasant smell. When the egg is released, this discharge will become heavier and more liquid – so you might notice it more for a few days. You then know your period will come 2 weeks later!

Most girls will start bleeding 6 months or so before they start ovulating. This is the reason some people believe that 'You can't get pregnant the first time you have sex'. In the old days, most girls didn't start their periods until they were 15 or 16 and might have got married before then. Sure enough, early sex didn't lead to pregnancy. Nowadays, we are healthier and both periods and ovulation start earlier, so this 'first time' myth is *not* one to believe!

Because periods were so frightening and mysterious to our ancestors, both men and women, we have all sorts of foolish stories about what you can and can't do when you are bleeding. For instance, some people still think you shouldn't have a bath or wash your hair. This is because everyone used to have baths together and men were terrified of having this strange, un-explained blood touching them, so women were forbidden to join in the bathing during their periods. Because you may feel unwell, and blood usually means a wound, women were often treated as if they were sick. This is also nonsense. You will find that exercise, warm baths and good food will help with any period pains, not make them worse.

Most young women have pain and cramps during their period and may feel headachy and sick in the week before. Some doctors will tell you it's all part of being a woman and that you'll have to put up with it. Others will be more helpful. If your periods give you trouble, it's worth asking your family doctor for help and advice.

If periods are the most obvious signal that puberty is well under way for a girl, the signal for a boy is his first wet dream.

Making a baby takes two – an egg from a woman and a sperm or seed from the man. Puberty gives boys the ability to repro-duce – or create new life – when they are around 13. Unlike girls, a boy is not born with his seeds already formed. When your hormones give the OK, your body begins to make these. Hang-

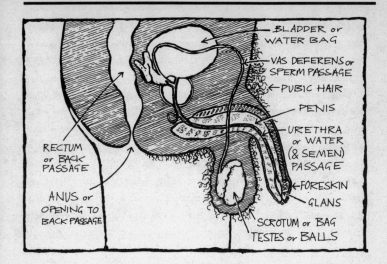

ing between your legs, boys and men have a penis – called by some a 'prick', 'cock' or 'willy' – and a bag containing two hard plum-shaped glands. These, the scrotum and testicles, are also known as the 'balls'. Before puberty, your penis and testicles are small. During puberty, they all increase in size. The testicles will start making minute, tadpole-shaped seeds called 'sperm'. As more are made, the sperm is forced along tubes until it

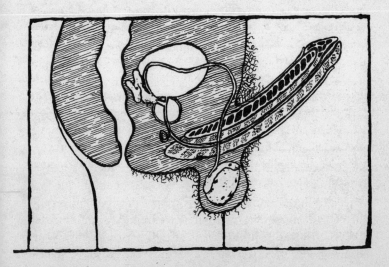

reaches a reservoir and is held. Sperm can stay there: eventually the body will soak it up or absorb it without doing you any harm. More usually, however, the body decides to get rid of the sperm by making you have an erection and a wet dream.

An erection is all part of getting you ready to make love, and we'll talk about this in another chapter! What happens is that your penis grows in size and becomes stiff. It will feel sensitive and you will find it extremely pleasant to touch and rub, both the shaft or main part and especially the head or 'glans'. But you can also feel pleasure without touching yourself at all – in a sexy dream. While you are asleep your penis will stand up and your dreams will be warm and exciting. You may dream of women – ones you know or film or pop stars. You may even dream of men – someone you admire perhaps. The result will be the same. You will wake up as a thick, white liquid spurts out of the tip of your penis where your urine or water usually come. This is called an orgasm, a 'climax' or 'coming'. It feels very pleasant. The fluid may seem to create an enormous puddle, but, in fact, you would find less than a teaspoon of liquid. Most of it is a fluid called 'semen', which keeps the tiny sperm safe and protected. There are about 300 million sperm in that teaspoon, by the way!

Having wet dreams is normal. It doesn't mean you are having 'impure' or nasty thoughts – the dreams are more a result of your body's need to push out the sperm than a reason for your erection. What is 'impure' about absolutely natural sexy feelings? We all have them!

You may also have erections at other times – at school, at a disco or in the street. An erection can be triggered off by the sight or thought of someone you fancy. Sometimes, they just happen for no obvious reason. It can be embarrassing, but other people will not notice as much as you think. You may think that you stick out a mile when, in fact, it's a small bulge easily hidden behind a book, bag or jacket.

However startling you may find these events, you must remember that you are not alone in experiencing them. Your friends will be going through the same stages, although it *is* quite normal to be a year or two behind the rest. *All* the adults

an involuntary erection can easily be hidden behind a book

you know – your parents, your teachers – will have gone through this too. If they aren't sympathetic and understanding, it's not because *you* are at fault, but because they have short memories or problems of their own. Don't struggle on alone.

Your Mum, an elder sister or a teacher will help you with periods. Your Mum won't tell you off for staining the sheets, so tell her in a straightforward way when you need a change because you've had a wet dream or 'leaked' during a period.

Remember, 48% of the population are male and have wet dreams and 52% are female and have periods. How can you be unusual?

3. The 9 Months Of Pregnancy

'I always wanted to have a baby when I was a kid. The whole thing just intrigued me and since my parents thought the facts of life were smutty, it took me ages to find out boys don't get pregnant! But I never did really satisfy my curiosity and I'm sure that's why I got my girlfriend pregnant in our second year at college' – John A.

Pregnancy is an event that fascinates us all. We all want to know where we came from and how we got here. Pregnancy is exciting and frightening for both boys and girls. Boys can be quite jealous of the mysterious power women have and long to know more about it. Girls can be thrilled at the thought of being able to create new life in their own bodies – but be nervous about the pain and mess they've been told to expect.

Some women are terrified at the very idea. Others, when they become pregnant, delay getting advice and even unwittingly harm their babies. This is usually because they don't know what happens during the 9 months of pregnancy.

A woman becomes pregnant when her egg and a man's sperm meet and join. This is called conception. This usually happens in one of the two tubes – called Fallopian tubes – which lead from her egg cases (or ovaries) to her womb. If the egg joins with one of the millions of sperm that swim up after each act of un-protected sex, it is said to be 'fertilized'; that is, it begins to grow into a baby. The fertilized egg travels down the tube to the womb, taking about 7 days to make the journey, and fastens itself to the wall of the womb. This is called 'implantation'. The egg sends out hormones, or chemical messengers, to stop the woman's body from having a period. This is because the lining of the womb, which is usually lost every month, becomes the home of the developing baby for the next 37 weeks. We normally

'FOR YEARS I THOUGHT BOYS COULD GET PREGNANT'

talk about pregnancy lasting 9 months. In fact, doctors and nurses count a pregnancy from the last day of the last period to the birth. This is usually 40 weeks. This timetable puts concep-

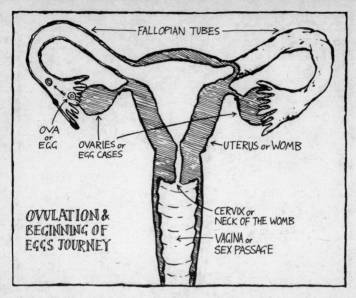

FALLOPIAN TUBES

OVA or EGG

OVARIES or EGG CASES

UTERUS or WOMB

OVULATION & BEGINNING OF EGGS JOURNEY

CERVIX or NECK OF THE WOMB

VAGINA or SEX PASSAGE

tion at the end of the second week and implantation at the end of the third.

Sometimes the egg will split after it has been fertilized and

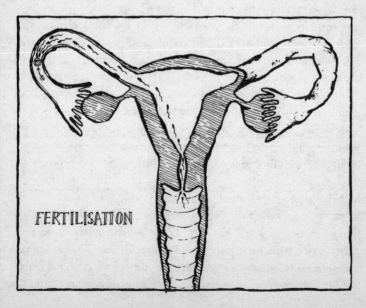

FERTILISATION

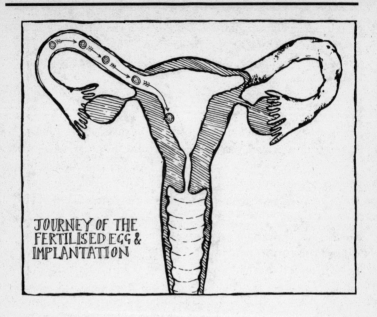

JOURNEY OF THE
FERTILISED EGG &
IMPLANTATION

develop into two babies. Since they came from the same egg and
the same sperm, they will have the same blood group and sex
and look alike. Twins can also be born if two eggs are released at
the same time and both fertilized. As the babies develop from
different eggs and sperm, they will only be as alike as any
brother or sister. They can be the same or different sexes, have
different blood groups and bear little resemblance to each other.
You have a greater than normal chance of having twins if a
female blood relative has already had twins.

Missing a period is the first sign of pregnancy for most
women. In the next few weeks their body starts adjusting to the
new lodger and various changes can be felt. Some women find
their breasts become bigger and softer, itch or feel tender.

The pink or brownish skin surrounding the nipples will
darken in colour and tiny goosebumps will show. A lot of
women have 'morning sickness'. This can happen because the
body is having to cope with changing levels of hormones.
Sometimes it is pure nervousness! In spite of all the tales, only
50% of pregnant women actually have morning sickness and it

usually stops after the third month. Hormone changes can also cause the mother-to-be to feel moody – swinging from happiness to sadness. Having a baby is an enormous step, so such feelings are only to be expected.

As soon as a woman thinks she is pregnant, she can have a pregnancy test. The chemical messengers the developing baby sends out can be found in a sample of her blood or, more usually, in her urine or water. You could take a sample to your doctor or clinic and they would do the test for free. Or you could buy a test at a chemist. The test bought over the counter can usually show whether you are pregnant as soon as you miss your first period. Doctors usually use a test that only shows up if you are two weeks late. By the time you have missed two periods, a doctor can tell you are pregnant by doing an internal examination. The doctor can feel that the womb is enlarged and becoming firm, while the cervix or opening to the womb is getting softer. Doctors can tell by the size of the womb how many weeks old the baby is.

Pregnant women should always go for ante-natal – that is, 'before birth' – care from their doctors as soon as they know they are pregnant. Most pregnancies are completely normal and cause no difficulties to mother or child. But 1 in every 3 women *do* have a problem which can almost always be cured by medical help and advice. Some women are more at risk. Young mothers who smoke or drink, do not eat a well-balanced diet or are overweight may find they and their babies are less healthy. At an ante-natal clinic, doctors and nurses will check that the baby is developing normally and is the right size for the dates. This is why it is important to know the date of the last period and so work out when the baby began. The doctor will check the health of the mother and discuss diet, rest and exercise. Pregnant women need plenty of rest – but they also need sensible exercise. The best form of exercise is swimming, which tones up the muscles without straining the body. Relaxing, warm baths also do an expectant mum a lot of good, soothing her and taking the weight off her legs and back. The doctor will keep a check on her weight and her blood pressure. Blood pressure is the force with which your heart has to beat to push blood around your body. If the force is greater than normal, the arteries and tubes carrying the blood thicken and narrow. The heart has to work too hard and wears out. Pregnancy can cause high blood pressure, so doctors watch this carefully. The doctor will also do a water or urine test, to check whether the mother might be diabetic. Diabetes is when your body is unable to use the glucose it processes from your food so instead of getting energy from your meals you get tired and sick. Pregnancy puts quite a strain on the body and could trigger this illness. They will also do a blood test to check that the mother is not anaemic nor has a venereal disease which could harm the baby.

After 9 weeks, the woman may find a thick yellow liquid oozing from her breasts. This is a special rich drink called colostrum that the baby drinks for a few days before milk is made. At 10 weeks, a doctor can feel the womb pulsing as the baby grows and moves. Up until now, the growing baby has been

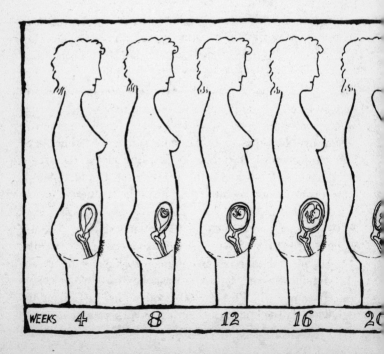

WEEKS 4   8   12   16   20

called an embryo. It has grown from a dot of cells hardly visible to the naked eye. As the vital organs and the limbs grow it changes from looking like a tadpole to a very odd looking lump with a bulge for a head, a tail and a spine running down the outside of its back. By the tenth week it begins to look human and is known as a foetus. By the thirteenth week it is obviously a human baby, although it is only 4 cms long.

Since the developing baby gets all its nourishment from the mother, anything she takes in may affect the baby. The umbilical cord – the link which carries blood and nourishment from mother to baby – can act as a filter and block out some germs and substances. But many will get through. For this reason, doctors strongly urge women to stop smoking and drinking while they are pregnant. Studies have shown that mothers who smoke have a greater chance of suffering a miscarriage or giving birth to a dead baby. A baby whose mother smoked in pregnancy is more likely to die in the first year of life, or be lighter in

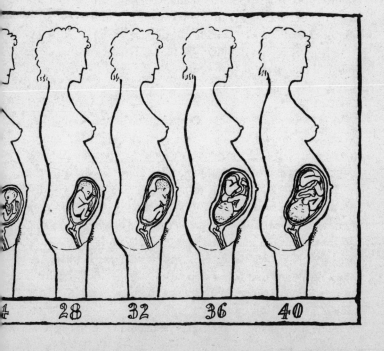

weight and suffer chest complaints. It is also thought that smokers' babies are more likely to be born with handicaps such as heart disease or hare-lips. Drinking in pregnancy can also affect the baby, and so can taking drugs. Illegal drugs such as cannabis, cocaine and heroin are obviously very bad for a baby – but even aspirin or antibiotics *can* do harm. The most famous example of this was the thalidomide tragedy. Mothers suffering from morning sickness were given this anti-vomiting drug. Not until too late was it realized that the effects on unborn babies hadn't been properly tested. Thalidomide didn't only prevent vomiting in the mothers, it acted on their babies in the vital first 3 months when the organs and limbs were forming. Many were born with arms or legs missing or only half-way formed. This is why doctors insist that a pregnant woman takes no drugs at all, stops smoking and cuts down her drinking. Some illnesses can pass from mother to child. The best known is Rubella or German Measles. To a child or even an adult, German Measles is a minor illness. A few spots, a touch of fever and a headache are all you'd probably feel. But if you caught this in the first three months of an unborn baby's life, the disease has far more dramatic effects on its development. Babies affected in this way can be born blind, deaf or with brain damage. This is why it is so vital to have Rubella immunization well before you plan to get pregnant.

During the fourth month, the baby and its protecting bag have grown enough to show. As the woman's belly swells, stretch marks appear on the skin which may remain after the birth. Some women also find a dark line may appear, from the navel or belly button down to the pubic hair. This will disappear after the birth. She may find she has to go to the loo more often, as the growing womb presses on her bladder – the long bag that stores her urine or water. Some women also develop varicose veins, when the veins in your leg become knobbly and show. You know that if you step on a hosepipe, the pressure of the water inside makes it swell. The foetus is doing the same thing to her arteries.

At this stage, some mothers may be offered an amniocentesis

test. The doctor gently pushes a needle through the wall of the belly and into the bag of fluid surrounding the baby, and draws off a sample. By testing the fluid, the doctor can tell if the baby is suffering from certain handicaps such as spina bifida or Down's Syndrome (mongolism). If it is discovered that the baby may be born severely handicapped, the parents and doctors can be prepared, or the mother may choose to have an abortion.

Between 17 to 20 weeks, the foetus 'quickens': its movements can be felt by the mother. During the next 20 weeks, the developing baby may stretch, punch and kick and move around inside the womb. You can see pregnant women suddenly start as they get a swift kick in the back or stomach . . . from the inside! If you watch a pregnant woman's belly carefully, you can actually see the bulges and ripples of movement. As the womb expands to hold the growing baby, it pushes upward into the body, displacing the other internal organs. The long bowel or gut which carries waste matter down to the back passage can get quite squashed, which is why pregnant women often suffer from constipation. Since the stomach is also squashed, she might find it uncomfortable to have a large meal. Little and often is the rule at the late stages of pregnancy. Eating for two, though, is a harmful old wives' tale, as a fat mother is an unhealthy mother. A growing baby actually needs only about 300 calories a day, so apart from making sure she is eating fresh food with plenty of vitamins and drinking fresh milk, most mothers do not need to change their diets.

At about 24 weeks the best known side-effect of pregnancy tends to appear – food craving. Food cravings can happen for two reasons. Some women will long for foods they particularly like. They may want to be spoiled and loved and so they ask their husbands to get them a special treat. Or it could be because the changes in hormones can affect taste buds and strong flavours like pickles or sour apples or very sweet puddings taste better than ordinary fruit or vegetables. In some cases, it can be because the growing foetus makes eating uncomfortable and she needs to be tempted. But many women crave the oddest things – and this is called 'pica'. Some eat soap or toothpaste, or clay or coal. Doctors point out that many odd food cravings are actually quite sensible. Pregnancy can use up a lot of essential minerals and vitamins, especially iron. If you are not getting enough, your body will find strange ways of making you eat a healthy ration. In most cases, pica is quite harmless, but some women do crave dangerous things such as disinfectant or fill themselves up with so much that they cannot eat the fresh foods they also need.

Dental care is very important during pregnancy since gums soften and can be harmed by rotting food. A good soft toothbrush and regular visits to the dentist are vital.

After 35 weeks, mother and baby start preparing for birth. Many women attend classes during their pregnancy – often with their husbands – where experienced teachers prepare them for giving birth. 'Natural childbirth' is a method which teaches women to relax during labour. Much of the pain of childbirth, say these teachers, is because of tension and fear. Armed with a knowledge of what is going to happen, the woman will be less tense and so have less pain.

The baby will now be lying head down in the womb. If it is not, the doctor will massage the womb and persuade it to move. The baby is big enough for the womb to stretch from the lower belly up to the ribs. The mother-to-be has to lean backwards when she walks (to keep her balance) and often has backache and needs to spread her legs and waddle. If this is her first pregnancy, with a month to go the baby's head drops down and can be felt lying just above the pubic bone. All through the pregnancy the womb has been contracting or flexing gently. Now it contracts every 15-30 minutes and starts forcing the baby out. All systems are go and the pregnancy is about to end – and a new life begin.

4. Giving Birth

'The idea of giving birth has always turned me off! But when I think about it, all I really know is hints and stories that I think aren't true. So it might not be as bad as all that!' – Trudy B.

The changes that happen in a woman's body in the 40 weeks from her last period to giving birth are dramatic but gradual. But birth brings even more dramatic changes in only a few hours.

The process of giving birth can take from 2 hours to 2 days. Unfortunately, films and books tend to make it seem like a very painful and unpleasant business. This terrifies many women and makes some decide never to become pregnant even though they long for a child. On the other hand, some people are so enthusiastic about the joys of birth that they can make you believe a woman will only feel pain if she fails to do the proper exercises, so women who *do* find it hurts feel guilty and think it was 'their fault'. Well, giving birth is hard work – it's not called being 'in labour' for nothing. But knowing what is going to happen, being fit, having toned up muscles and doing breathing exercises can certainly make it less of the harrowing experience it might be if you go ahead knotted up with fright and in total ignorance of what will happen.

What exactly does happen? All through pregnancy, the woman's womb pulses and flexes. Towards the end of the pregnancy, these ripples of movement get stronger and more frequent. When labour reaches the delivery stage, they will actually push the baby out of her. They are called 'contractions'. Sometimes a woman may think labour has started when in fact it is a false start. Before the contractions of the womb can actually push the baby out into the world, the cervix or opening to the womb must expand. The first signs of true labour are usually a deep ache in the back of the cervix which has, until then, kept tightly closed. It begins to soften and open. It has been blocked, for extra safety, with a 'plug' of body liquids and a little blood. As the cervix begins to expand, this plug will come out as a discharge. This is called the 'show'. The gradual opening of the cervix is the first stage of labour. During this period, contractions will come every 15 to 30 minutes and each will last for about 40 seconds.

When these early signs of labour begin, that is the time for the mum-to-be to grab her suitcase and head for the hospital in which her G.P. has booked her a bed. If she has arranged a home birth, she or a friend will call the midwife. This stage of labour can take from 1 hour to 24 hours, although in most births it takes from 8 to 12 hours.

On arriving at hospital, the woman is prepared for labour. The nurses or doctors check her pulse, blood pressure and a water sample to make sure all is well. Her belly will be examined to see how the baby is lying – head down or up. The baby's heart will also be listened for. In some hospitals the mum-to-be will have her pubic hair shaved. This is because some doctors still believe pubic hair can harbour germs and the baby may catch an infection as it comes out. Another reason is that if the mother has to have stitches afterwards, hair can get in the way. However, quite a few hospitals now accept that the itching caused by the hair as it grows back and the risks of infection from a shaving cut are worse than any chance of germs. And it can make you feel unhappy and strange.

It is important for the woman to empty her bowels or gut before going into the next stage of labour. This is because the pushing she will do to help the baby out could also cause her to open her bowels. Also, a full gut could actually block the womb's efforts to push. Some women have natural diarrhoea during the first stage but some need to be given help. She may be given a suppository – a 'tampon' shape of gel which is pushed up into her back passage – or the nurse may gently squirt up a syringe (no needles!) full of a solution to get things moving. In either case, after a few minutes, she will be rushing to the loo.

She is then invited to soak in a warm bath. This gets her clean, and, more important, allows the mother to relax and prepare for the next few hours of hard work: the second stage of labour, delivery.

Some women don't realize they have started labour until they reach this second stage. They can miss spotting the 'show', and don't notice the timing of contractions. This is rare, however, and stories of women giving birth in train carriages and the staff rooms of supermarkets are more because these women sped through to delivery rather than because they didn't realize it was happening. But certainly it *is* possible to sleep, read or generally go about as normal during the first stage. By the end of this stage, contractions will be coming every 2-5 minutes and lasting 40-90 seconds. They will be strong, for they are pushing the baby down against the opening of the womb. It may be painful as the thick and strong muscles are forced to relax and open. As the baby's head is pushed down, the thin membrane or skin that has covered and protected the opening will burst – just like a balloon full of water. The fluid, which looks and feels just like warm water, will gush out. The mother will have a strong urge to 'bear down' or push out the baby. If she finds it hurts, she can be given pain-killers. Many women prefer to remain clear-headed. In some cases the doctors suggest that a pain-killer may slow down the delivery or even affect the baby. Pain can be stopped with pills, or with a mixture of air and gas which the woman breathes through a mask as she requires it. Or she could have an 'epidural': a strong drug which is injected into the spine and knocks out all sensations below the waist, without making the woman feel 'woozy'. However, it does mean that she has to be lying on her side. She may also not be able to push hard enough and the baby may have to be helped out. Two out of every hundred women given an epidural do report a crashing headache the next day as a result.

There are various positions the woman can take to give birth. Your mother probably gave birth lying on her back or propped up. Nowadays, doctors realize that the 'primitive' ways of giving birth, where the woman squats or crouches, or stands, or is held under the arms by a medical person or friend or husband, make a lot of sense. If she is upright, gravity can help the baby out naturally. Many women find it much more comfortable to be upright. In the Middle Ages, they had 'birthing stools' – chairs with a cut-away seat which supported the back and buttocks but left space for the midwife to receive the baby as it 'dropped out'. Some modern hospitals are even reviving these stools!

The contractions of the womb and the mother's efforts will finally push the baby's head along the vagina or birth passage and out through her legs. This is called 'crowning' – as the crown or top of the head emerges. Although her body is very supple and built to stretch, in some cases the doctors may fear the opening will not quite be big enough and will tear. In these cases, a small cut is made. This is called an 'episiotomy'. It doesn't hurt at the time, although the stitches may sting or scratch afterwards. Some doctors now think that a small tear heals better than a cut. As the head comes out the mother can rest for a few minutes and the doctor or midwife will check to see that the umbilicus or cord is not wrapped round the baby's neck. Then the mother pushes again and the baby is born. This second stage of birth can take anything from a few minutes to one or two hours. The medical team will now quickly check that the baby is OK. They make sure he or she is breathing. Holding a baby up by its heels and slapping it is definitely a film or book myth, by the way! They will listen for a heartbeat, and check for active movement and response to a touch or sound. They will look at its colour. White-skinned babies are pale blue or mauve at birth but quickly turn pink as they breathe. Black babies are quite pale at first, so the change from blueish to pinkish is also noticeable. The team will add up a score for all of these things, and if the checklist falls below a certain score, a baby specialist will be called.

After a few minutes, the cord is cut and the baby is washed to clean away the blood and natural protective fluids which have covered it. Meanwhile, the mother will have been given an injection to make sure she stops bleeding and the placenta or afterbirth will be pushed out. This is the remains of the bag which fed and protected the baby in the womb. This is the final, third stage of labour. The mother is herself washed and dressed, and she and the new father (if he is present) will be left for a time with their new baby before they all have a well earned sleep.

In some cases, birth is not quite as simple. Sometimes, the bag of waters will not break and has to be painlessly burst. In some cases, the baby will not come out even when the waters have broken. A delay may put the baby at risk of an infection going up the birth passage. If the delay is because the contractions are not strong enough, the medical team might decide to 'induce' the birth. They will give the mother a drug, usually through a suppository in the vagina or a drip. A drip is a slow injection. A needle is put into her arm or into the back of her hand and a mixture of fluids 'drips' slowly into her bloodstream. This will encourage the womb to push. Very occasionally this is necessary because otherwise the mother may have given birth at an awkward time of the night or weekend when few staff are available to help her. In some cases, a normal birth is impossible and the baby is taken out with a 'Caesarean section'. This may happen if the woman has hips too narrow to allow the baby to pass. Or it could be because the team suddenly realizes that the baby is 'in distress'. This doesn't mean it's sad, but is in danger. The heart may have missed a beat or the baby was not getting enough oxygen. *Caesare* is the Latin for 'cut' – which is what happens. The woman is given an anaesthetic and a long cut is made through the stomach wall and into the womb. The baby is lifted out and looked after until the mother comes round.

In 95% of births, a baby is born headfirst. But in 5 out of every 100 births, the baby comes out face, bottom or even shoulder first. None of these should harm either the mother or the baby, although a shoulder-first baby may get stuck and have to be delivered by Caesarean section. But the medical team do have to work harder to make sure the baby comes out safely without being caught in the cord. In a few cases, a baby may stick half-way down the birth canal. If labour has been long, the mother can become so tired she can no longer push. In such cases, the medical team will use 'forceps'. These are instruments a bit like tongs, shaped to fit snugly but gently round the baby's skull. If it has travelled past the hips, these will be used to gently ease, but not pull, it out into the big, wide world.

In some cases, the baby may be ill at birth, or be born too early to be able to survive on its own. If so, he or she is put into a special unit, in an incubator. This is a bit like an artificial womb and keeps the baby warm, while tubes will give food and air. Having a baby whipped away immediately after birth can not only make a mother feel sad but can even make her feel the baby isn't hers when it is returned. Good hospitals now realize that mum and dad and baby must be able to see and touch each other as often and as much as possible after the birth.

Most mums will be up and about the day after giving birth, but some may be asked to stay in bed a bit longer or to take it easy. Depending on whether this is her first birth, how it went and whether she has help at home, the hospital will let her go home in a few days or a few weeks – there are no hard and fast rules.

Most new mums will go through a time of mood changes afterwards. They may feel wildly happy and then dreadfully weepy. Part of this is caused by the chemical changes in the body. Growing up – puberty – can have the same effect. Part, however, can be the sudden thought that this new scrap of life depends on her – an awesome responsibility. It can be worse if the new dad and family don't realize how tiring being a new mum can be. Having to get over giving birth *and* get up at all hours *and* do all the housework can get a bit much. This feeling of depression is called 'baby blues', and most mothers get it. Most will cheer up after a few days, but a few find it continues for ages. It is then called post-partum (or 'after birth') depression. Support and sympathy from the family and perhaps the family doctor should help. This depression can happen to mature, happily married women having chosen and planned babies. So it is easy to see how having a baby when you are unmarried, or too young, or have a rocky marriage, can end up in misery for everyone. Giving birth should be a wonderful, joyous occasion for everyone concerned – and it can be if you know what is going to happen and plan it for the right time in your life.

5. The Sting In The Tail

'I used to think life would be perfect when I grew up. It wasn't quite as simple as that. For a start, I suffered from Thrush through most of my teenage years. It made becoming a woman a trial rather than a pleasure' – Melanie N.

The parts of your body that give you sexual pleasure can also give you problems. Being a sexual adult and being a woman can carry a sting in the tail! Some of these problems will be triggered off by your having sex. Several, however, are just as likely to happen if you've never even kissed anyone!

The most common problems for girls are two infections. One is called Thrush, and affects your vagina or sex passage and the 'vulva' or fleshy area around it. The other is called Cystitis and affects your water passage or 'urethra'. Most young women are terrified if they develop anything wrong with these hidden, private parts of themselves. You can feel horribly shy and unwilling to talk to a doctor about these bits of your body. The thought of having somebody else examine you there is even worse, especially if your doctor is a man. You might also be afraid that the doctor will think you are 'dirty' and have been doing things you shouldn't. Whether you've had sex or not, this can be very offputting. Both of these conditions, however, can develop on their own, without any sexual contact. Thrush can affect any woman – 60-year-old maiden aunts, pregnant mothers, 13-year-old girls and day-old babies get it.

Our bodies are normally covered with, and are full of, bacteria. These are microscopic creatures which live in harmony with us. Thrush is an organism very like yeast, and it lives in your vagina absolutely harmlessly at most times. But, if the chemical balance of your body is upset, Thrush will suddenly multiply. The tiny organism responsible is called 'Candida

Albicans' – which is Latin for 'the glowing white whites'! It is so named because Thrush gives you white spots all over the surface of your vagina. You won't be able to see these, but you will find that you have a yeasty-smelling discharge from your vagina which looks almost like cottage cheese. Your vagina and the area around it may be swollen and itch maddeningly. If you ignored it, Thrush itself would not do you much harm, although you would be very uncomfortable. It could, in rare cases, be a symptom of another, more serious, disease. People who are developing Diabetes often get Thrush as a first symptom. So, it *is* worthwhile seeing your doctor just in case. The doctor would give you some cream to stop the itching on the outside. To clear up the Thrush in your vagina you would be given some cream 'pessaries'. These are tampon-shaped pieces of solid cream which you push gently into your vagina, where they cure the problem.

If you get a yellow, smelly discharge with no itching, you could have an infection. This can happen if you forget to take out your last tampon at the end of your period. Or you can damage the delicate tissue in the vagina with vaginal deodorants. These are *entirely* unnecessary and can be very bad for you. Some strong soaps can also harm you, as can disinfectants in bath water.

Another common problem for girls is Cystitis. This is sometimes called the 'honeymoon disease' because it can occur when a girl first has sex. Cystitis is an infection or inflammation of the bladder (the bag which holds your urine) or of the urethra – the tube that carries your water from the bladder to the front opening between your legs. When you have Cystitis, you want to pass water all the time, even when your bladder is empty. When you do go to the loo, your water may be blood-stained and smelly, and passing it will be painful. You may ache just above and to the side of your pubic hair and feel feverish. Cystitis may be caused by bruising the skin around the water opening, which can happen to a girl during early sex or clumsy petting. But, far more often, it is caused by tiny germs which inhabit your back passage finding their way into the front opening. This happens if you are a bit careless about hygiene or wipe yourself from the back to the front after going to the loo. To test for Cystitis, your doctor sends a water sample to the hospital and may then give you antibiotics. You could help yourself by drinking plenty of water – the more you have to pass, the less painful it will be. Drinking water with a teaspoon of bicarbonate of soda or barley water is even better. Lying down, with a hot water bottle against your back and one between your legs, also helps. Every time you go to the loo, you should wash between your legs with luke-warm water, but no soap.

Boys can get a similar infection, which in them is called Urethritis, or inflammation of the urethra. With them, how-ever, it is usually a result of having caught a Venereal or Sexually Transmitted disease. 'VD' or 'STDs', as most doctors like to call them now, are often used as a threat to put you off having sex. You can easily get the idea that VD is a punishment waiting to mark you if you do something wrong. 'Venereal' means 'linked to Venus', who was the goddess of Love.

VD is no more a punishment for sex than measles is for going outdoors! The fact that one is usually caught during slightly more intimate contact than standing next to a measles case in a bus queue is neither here nor there! You are more likely to catch VD if you have several partners, but promiscuous sex does not always lead to it, and having caught a form of VD does *not* mean the sex you had was loveless. In fact, you could 'catch a dose' on your wedding night as a virgin, from a virgin-except-for-one-encounter partner! But, just as you should avoid catching *any* illness, you should certainly avoid VD. There are 3 ways of doing so:

1) Don't have sex – a foolproof method if you can stick to it!
2) Stay faithful to one partner – or at least be picky about your partners.
3) Use a barrier method of contraception, such as a sheath.

The commonest forms of VD are Gonorrhoea and Syphilis in both men and women, Non-specific Urethritis in men and Tri-chomoniasis and Non-specific Vaginitis in women. 'Non-specific' means that the doctors can see that there is a problem, but cannot track down the germ causing it!

If you caught Gonorrhoea, you would probably notice a yellow discharge from your vagina or penis. You may have a burning pain when you go to the loo, and may feel aching and shivery. But women can sometimes be infected by the germs deep inside their bodies, in the tubes leading from the womb to the ovaries, and have no obvious symptoms. If Gonorrhoea is left untreated, it can so affect women's tubes or men's testicles that they may become unable to have children. Untreated Gonorrhoea can also lead to lasting pains in the joints.

Syphilis is rarer, but even more serious if left alone. If you caught this disease, you would start off with a tiny, painless sore on or in your vagina or penis. This would heal on its own. Sometime later, you would have a painless rash and feel generally unwell – as if you had 'flu. *Years* later, your heart, eyes, ears and nervous system would begin to show damage which cannot then be cured.

Non-specific Urethritis and Vaginitis show with discharge and pain on passing water.

All these diseases can be quickly, easily and *totally* cured AS LONG AS YOU GO FOR HELP AT ONCE! Most hospitals have a clinic specially to treat them. These clinics have different names. Some hospitals call them Special Clinics or STD Clinics or Genito-Urinary Departments or Venereology Departments. You can visit one without a letter from your doctor. The only thing they will ask you to do is to contact your sexual partner to get them treated too.

If you have a bad case of Thrush or Cystitis, your own doctor might send you to one of these clinics. This is *not* because he or she thinks you have a venereal disease, but because the hospital clinic has all the equipment and expertise to treat *any* illness affecting this part of your body.

There is one condition that can be passed on through sex that can't be cured at the moment. This is called AIDS – which stands for 'Acquired Immune Deficiency Syndrome'. AIDS is a *very* rare condition. It occurs when you have picked up – or 'acquired' – something that stops your body from defending itself against diseases. Normally, the body has an 'immune' system which kills germs and helps you fight illnesses. With AIDS, your immune system won't work – is 'deficient'. You can then get all sorts of skin cancers or lung infections and these are then called 'syndromes', or collections of illnesses.

AIDS has been called 'The Gay Plague'. It was first noticed in America, among homosexual men. However, this *doesn't* mean it is a punishment for gay sex, as some moralists have suggested. The total figure for reported cases in America was 17,000 by February 1986 – 287 in the UK. As an estimated 1 in 10 people are gay, it hardly appears as if making love to a member of your own sex automatically gives you AIDS!

Researchers are sure that AIDS *cannot* be spread by touch or through the air. Apart from gay men, the other 'high-risk' groups are drug addicts, both men and women, who share needles; sexual partners of drug users; and haemophiliacs – people whose blood doesn't clot properly and who need many blood transfusions. From this it would seem that the AIDS virus is spread by blood or semen, so the only way you could get it would be to have sex with a sufferer or have their blood get into your veins.

Symptoms which *might* suggest AIDS are swollen glands, unexplained and severe weight loss, skin rashes, discharges, diarrhoea, unexpected tiredness and breathlessness with a dry cough . . . all lasting for several weeks. However, if you have any of these, don't assume you have AIDS. See a doctor for reassurance by all means. But the chances of it being AIDS are minute!

Another sexual sting in the tail, of course, is pregnancy when you don't want it. Creating new life can be the most wonderful thing – as long as you and your partner are both at an age and a time of your lives when you want to be parents. If not, it can be a disaster.

A boy who gets a girlfriend pregnant has two choices. He can stick by and help her *or* he can be a louse and pretend it's nothing to do with him. Supporting the girl can be difficult. You may find that your parents are disappointed and hers are furious. You could find yourself shouted at by everyone and even beaten up by an angry father or brothers. If she is under 16, they may even ask the Police to punish you! Your girlfriend may be so upset that she blames you and says you persuaded her. This can happen particularly if her parents find it difficult to believe 'their little girl' actually wanted to make love. It can seem an easy option to run out on the situation. But do you want her – and her friends – to remember you as a little boy who couldn't handle the rough side of being grown up? However unpleasant, you'll feel better if you stick by her and take joint responsibility. You both made love, so you should both be involved in what happens afterwards.

In some cases, the boy *does* want to help and it is the girl, or more often her parents, who try to cut him out. In such a situation, you might like to get your parents or a trusted adult such as a teacher or youth club leader to help you make your case to her parents.

A girl who becomes unhappily pregnant has three choices. She can keep the baby. She can give it up for adoption. Or she can have an abortion. You can't force the boy to marry or keep you, but he can be made to contribute to the baby's upkeep after the birth. Looking after a baby is far more difficult than you think – we'll talk about being a parent in another chapter. It's not something to get into lightly. Having his child *won't* make a boy love you or force him to stay. Single parenthood can be a very great strain on both the girl and her parents, and on the baby. Giving a child away for adoption may seem a good choice, but this too can be agonizing. Having carried a baby for 9 months, you may feel as if a part of yourself has been taken away.

Although almost all young people say the thought of abortion – or 'getting rid of a baby' – horrifies them, nearly half the teenagers who become pregnant *do* choose this as the least of the evils. What happens in an abortion? At conception, you will be carrying within you a minute bundle of cells. This will grow into a baby. Modern religious opinion says it has a soul at conception, although it used to be believed that a soul entered a baby boy at 40 days and a girl at 80 days! Some religions believe the embryo to be a full being, to be protected from the beginning. Others choose various times during pregnancy at which the baby begins to be considered as important as the mother. Certainly, the medical fact is that a baby cannot survive outside its mother before 22 to 28 weeks, when the lungs have finished growing. The law in this country is that if two doctors agree that a woman both wants and needs an abortion before the baby can survive on its own, an abortion can be performed. The doctors can decide this if they think the pregnancy would do more harm to the woman or any existing children than the abortion. They can also give her an abortion if they believe that the baby may be born handicapped.

Up until 12 weeks, the embryo does not look like a baby. It has grown from a few cells to a lump with growing organs and stumpy legs and arms. At 12 weeks, it is two inches long and weighs a third of an ounce. A doctor can do a 'D & E' or a 'D & C' to abort the pregnancy. In a 'D & E', or Dilation and Evacuation, he will give the woman an anaesthetic to put her to sleep. A thin, metal instrument is used to 'dilate' or widen the entrance to the womb. Then a thin, plastic tube is passed inside and the lining of the womb and the tiny developing embryo is sucked out. In a 'D & C', or Dilation and Curettage, a thin, spoon-shaped instrument is used to gently scrape the lining and embryo from the womb.

Between 12 and 15 weeks the developing baby, now called a 'foetus', grows an inch in length and a sixth of an ounce. It begins to look more like a baby but is still smaller than your index finger. During this time, a doctor would have to do a 'D & C'. After 15 weeks, the foetus is too large to pull through the entrance to the womb without hurting the woman. So the doctors would have to wait a few weeks until the pregnancy had got to the stage when the entrance to the womb is ready to relax and open up. At this stage, an abortion is done by making the woman's body have a miscarriage, or push the baby out as it would at childbirth, but before the baby is ready to emerge. A 16- to 20-week-old foetus could be between 7 and 10 inches long and weigh between 4 and 12 ounces. This sort of abortion is very unpleasant for both the woman and the medical staff. For a start, as she is in effect giving birth, and before her body is fully ready, it will probably be painful. If she is given painkillers, this would slow it down, so she usually has to grit her teeth and bear it. Although the foetus is tiny – weighing less than a pack of butter – it still looks like a miniature baby. Although it can't survive, it may still wriggle and make sounds as it comes out. This can be very upsetting for everyone.

Early abortions are, however, painless and very safe. It is not true that an abortion will make you sterile – as long as you do *not* try to do one yourself, but go to a doctor. Your own doctor, or a doctor in a family planning or youth advisory clinic, would help you if you needed it. As long as you were under 12 weeks pregnant you could be sent to a NHS hospital and not have to pay. Between 12 and 20 weeks pregnant, you might have to go to one of the pregnancy charities. Even though the law allows for abortions up until 28 weeks *or* until the baby can live on its own (nowadays, with better care, this varies from between 22 to 28 weeks) you will find it *very* rare that a doctor will help after 20 weeks.

It all sounds very unpleasant, but the women who choose abortion rarely do so lightly. They are just like you or me – not callous, cold or heartless, as some people say. They weigh up the choices and decide that abortion is not a perfect but the most acceptable solution for the majority of people involved.

Nobody can force an abortion on you, or stop you having one if your doctors agree with you. Even if you are under 16, your parents cannot insist, nor can a husband or boyfriend. So, speak up and make your feelings known to the doctors! If you are under 16, your parents must, of course, be involved. But, in the end, it is your life and your decision that matters.

6. Better Safe Than Sorry

'**A** friend of mine got pregnant in the fourth form. She had a really rough time, so I wasn't going to let that happen to me. We talked, Geoff and me, and he came with me to the clinic. It wasn't the nicest hour I've ever spent – but I was so relieved after. When I told my mum where we'd been, she was a bit shocked. But after, she said she was also relieved that we'd been sensible' – Kate F.

Having a baby can be wonderful. But if both partners are not ready for the enormous responsibility or already have the children they want, it can be a disaster for everybody. If you were married in your early 20s and only wanted 2 children, you would have over *20* years of wanting to have sex while protected from pregnancy. If, like most people, you start your sex life before marriage, you have even more reason for wanting to know about birth control.

There are several methods of stopping a pregnancy. There are also some unsafe ones! The methods you shouldn't rely on are 'being careful' or withdrawal; the 'Safe' Period or Rhythm Method; or crossing your fingers and hoping for the best! 'Being careful' is often bandied about as a good method. People who'll say they use it often don't actually know what it means. It *doesn't* mean just hoping. It means a boy pulling out his penis from a woman's vagina before he 'comes', and having his orgasm outside her. The idea is that the sperm then don't have a chance to reach the egg. Sadly, this is not always true. Sperm can leak out with the fluid that makes sex comfortable while you make love. By the time you pull out, sperm are already swimming on their way.

The 'safe period' or 'rhythm method' is based on the fact that only one egg is released each month. The idea is that you can

USELESS METHOD OF CONTRACEPTION Nº 625
~ JUMPING UP & DOWN AFTERWARDS
[usually recommended for female of couple]

chart when ovulation – the release of an egg – is likely to happen, avoid sex at this time and enjoy it at others. The only problem is that, as we've seen, you really can't be sure this will work. One family planning expert is fond of saying: 'There's a name for people who use the rhythm method – parents!' It can be fairly successful if a couple work very hard at it. A happily married couple who wouldn't really mind if a baby arrived could find it a good way of delaying a pregnancy, but it's no easy option for young lovers.

Safe methods include the Pill and Mini-Pill, the Coil (also known as the loop or IUCD) and the 'sheath'.

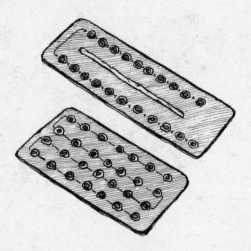

The Pill, or Combined Oral Contraceptive Pill, contains man-made hormones like the ones produced by your body during pregnancy. When you take the Pill, your body is fooled and thinks you are pregnant. You take a tablet every day for 3 weeks and then have 7 pill-free days. During this week, your period will come. You then begin a new packet. As long as you keep to the routine, never missing a pill and beginning the next packet on time, your body will not release an egg, so you can't get pregnant. Some women on the Pill put on weight, feel depressed or sick – just as some have these problems when they get pregnant. They are called 'side effects'. There are also medical reasons why you may not be able to use the Pill. If any blood relatives have had certain illnesses such as heart attacks or blood clots in the veins (also called coronaries and thrombosis), a doctor may decide that you are at risk of developing these, since the Pill

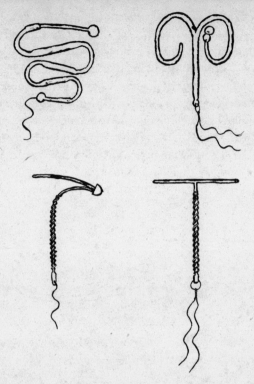

adds to this risk. Smoking and being overweight increase these risks, too. Taking certain drugs such as long courses of antibiotics or being sick and having diarrhoea can cancel the effect of the Pill. But if you take it properly, you cannot get pregnant.

There is a type of Pill – the Progestogen only Pill or Mini-Pill – which has no side effects and will do no harm. However, it is slightly less safe than the Combined Pill, and for every 100 women taking it over a year, 2 to 5 may become pregnant.

The Coil or loop is properly called an Intrauterine Contraceptive Device or IUCD. This means an 'in the womb baby-stopping thingy'! A trained doctor or nurse puts a specially made piece of plastic and copper in your womb. These pieces are shaped like a '7' or a 'T' or a double 'S'. The early IUCDs were coils of metal – hence the name!

As it sits there, the IUCD affects the womb in such a way that it refuses to allow an egg to implant in the lining. Once you've had an IUCD fitted, you only need to check for yourself that it's still there after your period every month. Women who have never been pregnant sometimes find an IUCD gives them cramps, pains and heavy periods. They can also increase your chances of developing an infection. For this reason, doctors are unhappy about giving them to young people.

The Pill and the IUCD work by either stopping an egg being produced or not allowing it to implant in the womb. Another method of stopping pregnancy is to prevent sperm and egg from meeting. A woman can wear a 'Cap' or diaphragm to do this.

The Cap is a dome of rubber with a flexible rim. The woman squeezes it into a tampon shape and then slides it up into her sex passage. The Cap opens out and fits snugly over the entrance to the womb. This lies near the end of her sex passage. For extra safety, she puts a cream or jelly on the Cap. This is called spermicide or sperm killer. When the man 'comes', his sperm is held back from going into the womb, while the cream kills it. The cream is harmless to anything but sperm, by the way!

You can have the same effect if the man wears a 'sheath' or condom. [These are also called 'dunkies', 'jolly bags', 'Durex'

'French letters' or even 'wellies'.] They are bags made of very thin, flexible rubber and are unrolled over the erect penis. When he comes, the man's sperm is held in the end. Some men say: 'It's like taking a bath with your wellies on' (hence one of the names). They claim you can't feel anything wearing one and that this spoils sex. In fact, they are so thin that you can hardly feel much difference – certainly not enough to make an unwanted pregnancy a better option! Many boys use this as an excuse, when actually they are afraid of looking inexperienced or even of losing their erection as they try to put one on.

You can buy sheaths at a chemist or from slot machines, or

get them free from a Family Planning Clinic. A woman must get the other methods from a doctor. She can see her own family doctor or someone at a Family Planning Clinic or a Youth Advisory Centre. Many girls risk pregnancy because they are afraid of what will happen when they see a doctor for birth control.

You can ask for a doctor's advice and help about this *whatever* your age. If you are a girl under 16, your boyfriend is breaking the law if he has sex with you. The law that says this was made to stop young girls being sold as prostitutes to old men. It wasn't made to stop young lovers showing their affection. For this reason, the girl is not breaking the law, and neither is a doctor who helps her. The doctor *is* within his rights to refuse to give you birth control and to try to talk you out of doing anything. He would also be doing the right thing if he asked *you* to speak to your parents, but he should not 'tell on you' to your parents without your say-so.

Your early steps in love are something you might not want to discuss immediately with your parents, whether you are a girl or boy. This isn't being deceitful, nor is it 'going behind their backs'. You wouldn't want them telling you about their sex life, would you? Just as you would expect them to have private areas in their lives, so you might want to keep this as your own. The point about being an adult is that you break away from your parents' all-embracing care. But you should recognize that they will want to know and share what is happening to you. With some parents, it is out of jealousy and a refusal to accept that you are no longer a child. With most, however, it is out of a very real wish to love you and to protect you from harm. By all means keep your *privacy*, but try not to let it become *secrecy*. The more honest and open you are with your parents, the more they will trust, and accept that you are growing up.

The doctor will ask a woman requesting birth control a lot of questions, whatever your age. And however strange they may seem, there is a reason for all of them. You may need to explain about your and your family's health, when you started having periods, if you smoke and much else. You *must* be honest – a lie could mean that the doctor gives you something that harms you.

If you have not yet had sex, you may not need to have an Internal at once. But, if you have, or are going to use a Cap or an IUCD, this will be necessary for every woman.

An 'internal' or 'vaginal' examination can be a bit uncomfortable. But unless you are really tense and uncooperative, it will *not* hurt. What happens is this. The doctor will ask you to remove your lower clothes and lie on the couch with your knees raised. He or she will then take an instrument called a 'speculum'. This is made of plastic or metal and looks like two spoons with long flat bowls hinged together. Nice doctors will make sure it's warm! Having put some cream on the end to make it slippery, the doctor will very carefully guide the instrument into your vagina. Your vagina, however small it may seem to you, is a very flexible tube of flesh and muscle. Remember that at some time in your life it may have to stretch to let pass up to 10 pounds of baby. When the speculum has been gently guided into you, the doctor eases the two halves of it apart. He can then see up to the top of the vagina, where the neck of the womb – the cervix – juts into the passage. He can examine the sides of the vagina and make sure they look healthy. He can see the cervix to make sure that it is a good pink colour with no signs of damage or infection. At this point, he may take a 'smear' test. This is not as painful as it sounds. Your body sheds cells all the time – next time you have a bath, scrub your arms and see the amount of 'dead' skin that comes away in what looks like dirt. All the doctor does is carefully guide a smooth, thin wooden instrument the size of an ice-lolly stick up between the halves of the speculum and collects some cells from the cervix and the walls of the vagina. You may not feel a thing because we do not have many nerves at the top of the vagina, only at the bottom. This is why a tampon can hardly be felt when it is in place. The doctor has the sample of cells looked at to see if you are developing cancer of the cervix. This is a type of cancer that can happen to young women – especially if they have early sex. Cancer does not happen overnight. The cells change gradually from healthy to cancerous. If you have regular smears, your doctor can tell very early on if you've developed this disease, and cure it quickly, easily and painlessly. If cancer is left until it causes pain and bleeding, it may be too late.

The speculum is then taken out and the doctor will now do what is called a 'bimanual' or two-handed examination. If you can imagine what it is like feeling around inside a cloth bag while wearing gloves and trying to work out which object is your pen, keys or purse, you can see what he is trying to do. The doctor puts two fingers into your vagina and the other hand on to the outside of your stomach or abdomen. By pressing his hands towards each other, he can feel your womb and your ovaries through the skin, flesh and muscles that comes in the way. With experience and practice, a doctor will be able to tell if everything is in place and whether there are any lumps, bumps or bits that shouldn't be there. He can also tell from the feel of the womb whether you are pregnant and, from the size, how many weeks on. *Very* occasionally, he may even have to put his finger in your rectum or back passage, if he needs to feel further up into the body than the vagina goes.

None of this will be painful, unless you are so nervous and unhappy that you scrunch up your muscles so that he has to push hard to make any headway. The trick is to lie back, relax and keep saying: 'It will be all over in a minute and it *is* doing me good.' When a woman is visiting her doctor regularly for birth control, she will be offered these smear tests as a routine check-up. The doctor may also do a breast examination, which can be a bit embarrassing if you don't know what the doctor is looking for and why he does it. Your breast is made up of fat, tissue and tiny tubes which would produce and carry milk if you got pregnant. Sometimes, tiny lumps form in the tissue. These could just be blockages in the tubes, or these could be small cysts or a growth of fibrous tissue. All these can be painful, but are essentially harmless and can be removed easily. But some lumps are more serious – they can be signs that the woman has breast cancer. Cancer lumps are usually painless, which is why women who find a lump and are scared will persuade themselves 'it's nothing', believing that if there is no pain, there is no problem. Breast cancer usually strikes women over the age of 30, so you might well think it is unnecessary for you to have to bother with such an examination, but you are wrong. Cancer *can* affect a very few young people, and regular examinations would reveal any changes *immediately*. Cancer *can* be cured totally if it is caught in the early stages. To check for small lumps, your doctor will 'palpate' your breasts, systematically press the flat of his fingers over your breast to feel the tissues under the skin. He may also ask you to stand in front of him and to raise your arms. Some bumps are too tiny to feel but will show up by making the skin above them dimple when you do this. He would also examine your nipples. If these weep blood or pus, or if a nipple which normally sticks out turns suddenly inwards, this could signal a breast problem.

If you are going to use a Cap, the doctor will try out several sizes to choose the right one. He will then ask you to practise putting it in and pulling it out with your index finger. If you are to have an IUCD, he would also use a thin, plastic rod to pass up your vagina and into your womb to measure the length of the womb. He then introduces the device into your womb through a small, hollow rod.

If this all sounds offputting, think of it this way. Using birth control is the price you must pay if you want sex without a baby. You have three choices:

1) Sex and baby
2) Sex and birth control
3) No sex!

If the first would cause distress and you can't face the second, then the only responsible and mature choice is the third. The only people who opt for the first are those who are adult enough to *want* to become parents and *understand* the responsibilities; or silly kids who don't know what they are letting themselves in for and won't face up to reality.

7. Friends And More

''ve got two great mates, and they're far more important to me than boys. I'd let a boy down before I'd dump on them – and they're the same to me. Friends are the best thing you've got!' – Maggie F.

What is a friend? Someone you can have a laugh with? Someone you tell all your secrets, share your thoughts, lend your clothes?

We have friends from very early childhood. Some of us like having a 'special', best friend and others prefer being part of a group. Whichever you choose, the chances are that puberty will bring changes to your patterns of friendship. You may now demand more of your friends, and have to offer more to keep the relationship.

This becomes particularly important because as your body alters and adjusts to being that of an adult instead of a child, your emotions will also need to prepare for having an adult sexual relationship. The sort of love or liking you have felt for relatives and playmates is joined by a new type of feeling, that of sexual interest. But, as with many new games, you have to practise first, so nearly everyone goes through a phase where they get crushes and infatuations on people. These can strain the best friendship!

Teenage crushes are very often for someone of the same sex. The person you are attracted to may be a teacher or prefect at your school, a youth or social worker at a club, a friend's brother or sister or even a friend of your own. You'll find seeing and listening to them gives you a jumpy sense of excitement and pleasure. You may dream and daydream about them. This is absolutely normal and doesn't mean you have an 'unnatural' liking for your own sex – we'll talk about this in another chapter. Very few people, if they are honest, do not have these feelings.

At the same time, you may find yourself 'falling in love' with someone you don't know at all – a pop or film star, or someone you often see on television or in a magazine. You may become 'infatuated', and spend time weaving imaginary stories around them. Being out of reach gives them that safe glamour – your dreams can be as outrageous as you want and you don't have to face them next day! As with a crush, the dreams and longings you have for a person you love from a distance are both good and normal. They give you a chance to explore, and get used to, all those new, adult sensations and emotions.

Such an attraction sometimes happens because, without knowing it, you are trying to work out what sort of person you want to be when you are older. Experts call this finding a 'role model'. It means you admire and want to copy the person, and will model your behaviour on theirs. You might choose a popular, successful person or you might also show anger and rebellion by choosing someone exciting and different, that your parents would hate.

Your feelings will be strong and very real, and nobody should sneer at them. But there should come a point when you recognize that they *are* practice rather than the true thing, because a relationship and love can only be genuine if it's two-sided.

An infatuation can get badly out of hand if you fall for an older person of the other sex, such as a teacher, a friend of your parents or a neighbour. The problem is that you may make your interest very obvious. And since you will probably look and act like an adult in their eyes, they may respond in kind. It may sound exciting to have a relationship with a grown-up – the reality will be *very* different. If he or she *is* an honest and decent person who really feels deeply for you and wants to go on being with you, it may well lead to their losing their job, their family and their friends. More likely, they will be someone to whom it will just be a selfish game that will leave you very hurt.

You may find that none of this affects your day-to-day friendships. Indeed, several of you may share the same crush on a teacher or love for a film star, and part of the fun will be competing for attention or going to films or concerts together. The trouble starts when you become ready to shift your attention to a real boy or girl.

Since most boys start puberty a year or two after girls, you may find you are attracted to someone with a year or so age difference. But there *are* a few early and late starters, so don't let the fact that you are in the same year put you off! The main problem is that many people think that someone who hasn't a boy or girlfriend is 'funny' or a failure. So being the first – or, at least, not the last – in your crowd to prove yourself suddenly becomes important.

We all develop at different rates. Some of us want to explore friendships with the opposite sex at an age when others are still quite content to play around. Or a special person we'd like to spend time with comes on the scene and they just happen to be of the opposite sex. The sad thing about seeing boys and girls as just 'boyfriends' or 'girlfriends' is that you often treat them as an object or a means of showing off, and forget they're a person too! Someone of the other sex can be a *friend*, without any sexual overtones at all. A lot of young people find themselves pushed into something neither of them wants because they forget this. 90% of what you hear from your crowd at this time is likely to be fantasy or downright lies. Many a girl has wound up pregnant and many a boy an unwilling father because they thought everyone else was 'doing it'. Then they find they're the first of their friends to lose their virginity, after all!

When you do start going out with a boy or girl, it's often a great temptation to turn your back on your friends. After all, who needs them now you've got him or her? The answer is simple, *you* do! Friends forgive you after a row, friends put up with little differences of opinion. Friends are easy to be with – you don't have to look your best or make an effort. The only thing a good friend demands is your loyalty. This means you should not tell lies, tell tales or let them down. It's not much to ask, or give! But a boy- or girlfriend may break up with you over something very small – or the first flame of interest may just die down. You'll need your friends to pick you up, dust you off and tell you that you are still a worthwhile person. But they may not be there to help you if you've junked them in favour of the loved one. So, keep to a few sensible rules – for your own sake!

1) Don't break a date with a friend if your new boyfriend or girlfriend asks you out instead. You may think this proves you're in love – it doesn't! It just proves that you are prepared to be a louse and a doormat, and who can trust anyone like that?

2) Don't bore your friends with tales of how marvellous He or She is. You'll look pretty silly if it busts up next day.

3) Don't stretch the truth and give the impression you've experienced things when you have not. Especially don't say you've had sex when you haven't. Tall stories have a way of rebounding on you, and you'll feel guilty if a friend is pushed into copying you and really winds up in trouble.

Friendship can be pretty intense during your teenage years. This is the time when all of you are testing and exploring your world. You no longer want to accept without question the things your parents and other adults tell you. Your friends' opinions

DON'T BORE YOUR FRIENDS WITH TALES OF HOW MARVELLOUS S/HE IS

become more important to you than those of your parents, and your parents can find this very upsetting. You may find them criticizing your mates, often for petty things you feel are silly. Does it *matter* that so-and-so has dyed hair, pierced ears or scruffy jeans, swears or isn't polite? You like them because you think alike, can have fun together and get into really interesting discussions about Life, the Universe and Everything. In fact, Mum and Dad won't realize themselves that *appearance* is not really what annoys them. They are naturally jealous of the fact that your friends now come first. And this *hurts*!

It may hurt even more if you take any problems you may have to an adult other than them. Many parents become angry at the thought that their 'children' can, and sometimes do, go to professionals or just other adults for help. However, during these years there may be many problems you need to talk over without going to your parents. The point is, you are learning how to solve your own problems. You are preparing for separation – for leaving the safe protection of your parents' arms. It's not that you want to go behind their backs. It's that the whole point of these problems and questions is that you want to solve them without 'Mummy's and Daddy's' help!

But you *do* sometimes want the special knowledge or advice of an adult. Some teenagers have a 'chosen adult' at this time. It may be a teacher or youth club leader. It may be a neighbour or a friend's parent. It may be an aunt, uncle or grandparent, or even a much older brother or sister. You can ask their advice or opinion and know they won't tell you off or insist on anything, as you may feel your parents would. Parents have watched you grow up and often take you for granted. The very time when you have a vitally important question to ask, they may well rush off to wash the car or start supper. A chosen adult may well listen and treat you with proper, adult courtesy and respect.

You shouldn't be made to feel you have betrayed anyone if you *do* go to an outsider for such help, or find them easier to talk to than your own Mum or Dad. It doesn't mean either you or they have done anything wrong. It's just a fact that teenagers and their parents *do* find it difficult to communicate. Tell them you still love them – which you *do*! – and try to share some of your thoughts with them. In time, you will both be able to relax and get on, usually *after* the storms of the teenage years have gone!

8. The First Steps In Love

'**A**ll I heard from my parents were warnings – don't touch yourself, don't let boys mess around with you, don't do this and don't do that. What they never told me was how nice it could be and how I'd *want* to do it!' – Joan T.

The first steps in love can happen a long time before you are a teenager or find a person you fancy. It used to be called 'self-abuse', but a better name would be 'self-love'. You may have heard the word 'masturbation'. You may also have heard about 'wanking' or 'tossing off'. They all mean the same thing – touching your sexual organs to give yourself pleasure.

Nearly all human beings masturbate at some time in their lives. It is a pity that such a common, harmless and pleasant act is surrounded by so many cruel and stupid myths. Masturbation WILL NOT:

> Drive you mad
> Make you sick
> Make you weak
> Grow hair on your palms
> Enlarge
>> Shrink
>>> or deform your sexual organs.

You can't tell by looking or talking to anyone whether they have masturbated.

So what is masturbation? You will probably have been touching yourself for as long as you can remember. Babies explore themselves from curiosity. They soon find that it feels nice to stroke and rub certain parts. Toes and noses feel nice – lips, nipples and sexual parts feel even better. Some babies and toddlers can bring themselves to a peak of pleasure by rubbing these parts or by rocking to and fro. In most cases, though, it is at the start of puberty that this becomes a major source of pleasure for both sexes.

You may have felt the first stirrings of sexual excitement because of seeing, or thinking or dreaming about, someone you fancy – a pop star or actor or someone you have a 'crush' on. Or it may just be that you are stroking yourself for the nice feelings it brings. Whatever the reason, sexual excitement is the same. Your heart may beat faster. Blood will rush to parts of your body such as face, hands, breasts, and genital organs. They will feel warm and even sweaty. If you looked in a mirror, you would see that the pupils of your eyes are larger than normal and your cheeks and lips are red. This, by the way, is why women wear make-up – it makes them look sexually excited and exciting! And this is why candle light is romantic – it also enlarges your pupils.

At the same time, the juices in a girl's sex passage will start to flow, so her pants may be wet and stained with a clear or sticky white fluid. The lips surrounding her sex passage will swell and also flush red. Boys will find their penis swells with blood and stands out from the body. This is often called 'having a hard-on' or 'having the horn'. The testicles or balls also swell, so that the loose scrotum or sack they hang in appears to tighten. Boys will often find a clear or sticky white fluid oozes from the opening of the penis. Both may have a strange tingling feeling, almost as if they want to pass water! Both will want to masturbate.

In masturbation, girls may caress their sexual organs, around the vagina and the fleshy lips or labia. The most sensitive area is a little nub of flesh called the clitoris. This is found at the front of the slit of skin that enfolds a girl's water and sex passages. Boys concentrate on their penis, especially on the glans or head. In fact, in an 8-week-old unborn baby, the clitoris and the glans of the penis are the same organs. So the feelings a boy or girl has when stroking these parts are very similar. Rubbing them gives you a warm and comfortable feeling. It can also give you a gradually building up sensation of excitement and tension. This spreads through your body and suddenly explodes in a wave of tingly pleasure. It's a bit like a giant sneeze that affects your whole body. This is called an 'orgasm' or a climax. You may also hear it called 'coming'. When this happens to a boy, a sticky white liquid will spurt or ooze out of his penis. This is called semen, although you may have heard it called 'spunk'. Some girls find they can pleasure themselves to orgasm by squeezing their thighs together or holding a pillow or some other soft object between their legs. Boys will sometimes rub against a mattress or pillow. Both may find riding a horse or bicycle gives a pleasurable sensation. Both boys and girls may find they have exciting dreams about people they fancy. Sometimes, you even dream about people you think you can't stand or certainly haven't thought about as sexy! You can't always remember those dreams exactly, but wake up just as your body reaches orgasm. The dream can be so exciting that this happens without your needing to touch yourself.

Some people find the thought of masturbation alarming. Because it gives you a nice relaxed feeling afterwards, they fear it 'weakens' you. Some coaches still forbid their athletes to have any sort of sex before a game or race. Most modern coaches say the opposite – that release of sexual tension is relaxing and can be good for you. The fluid you produce at climax and during sexual excitement is not something your body needs to keep. It used to be believed that for a boy to lose semen – his 'spunk' – was as bad as losing a pint of blood. This is nonsense.

Most experts now agree that, far from being harmful, youthful exploration and pleasuring are a very important part of growing up. If you have awakened your body's ability to feel pleasure and know what gives you excitement, you can respond all the better with a partner when you are ready to have an adult relationship. Believing that masturbation will addict you to solitary pleasure is as silly as saying you'll never be able to play tennis with a partner if you start off knocking a ball against a wall!

It is quite natural to want to extend your explorations to another person's body. Children play 'doctors and nurses' to satisfy their curiosity about how other bodies *look*. Teenagers are also curious about how another person *reacts* and *feels*. But curiosity is not the only reason. Another is that when you feel liking or love for someone, you want to show it by giving them pleasure and getting as close to them as possible. This may lead you to what many people call 'necking', 'petting' and 'heavy petting'.

'Necking' is when you and your partner kiss and caress each other through your clothes and don't actually touch each other's sexual organs. Kissing can be just the touching of lips, or you may want to open the lips slightly and allow your tongues to stroke lightly.

Lots of girls and boys get really desperate about the idea of a first kiss. Will I do it properly? Will he or she know that I am a beginner? Will I make a fool of myself? Kissing *isn't* an Olympic event with gold medals for 'doing it right'. Nor is any part of sex for that matter. You don't have to know or learn how to kiss. The point about a kiss is that it is just another way of stroking, patting, or hugging your partner; what comes naturally is right. You may lean against someone you like, but want to hold and smother someone you really go for. The same applies with a kiss. You'll want to offer a light pressure of lips to one person, but open your mouth and offer more to another.

Some people think that a 'French kiss' – one where the tongues meet or thrust into each other's mouths – is a signal that the other person wants sex. This may be so. Plunging a tongue into a mouth is similar in a way to the action of intercourse. And such kissing can be part of sexual excitement, so one or both of you may want to go further at this point. But it *needn't* mean this. You don't have to feel either of you *has* to do anything further just because you've French kissed.

Necking can also involve the stroking of breasts through clothing. Boys tend to be fascinated by breasts and find them as pleasant and exciting to stroke as girls find them to be stroked. What fewer people realize is that *boys'* nipples are as sensitive and that it's just as nice for the boy if she, too, touches him there.

'Petting' is the next stage, when genitals are often touched through clothing and the boy touches the girl's breasts under her bra or top. She may even strip to the waist. In heavy petting, both touch each other's sexual organs and even bring each other to orgasm. Both may choose to strip off entirely – but not actually have full sex. When you neck or pet you will find the strangest parts of your body become sensitive and feel nice when touched. Your neck, shoulders, ears, fingers, inside of elbows, wrists and knees and toes as well as the obvious lips and breasts will tingle and react if stroked. Parts of your body that feel nice when touched in this way are often called 'erogenous zones'. This is from the god of Love – Eros, so it means loving or sexy areas.

Whether you're necking, petting or heavy petting, you may acquire love bites. Love bites are bruises, which can happen quite easily when you suck hard on the skin, rather than actually sinking your teeth in! Love bites happen because you both get carried away with kissing. You're trying to show your intense feelings and neither of you realize how strongly you are attacking each other. More often, love bites are a way of showing off. Brandishing your scars, you can prove to friends that you and your boy- or girlfriend are 'doing it'. They're also a way of flaunting in your parents' and other adult faces that you're no longer a child but a very sexy adult.

You may have heard people talk about 'fingering' and 'having a feel' or 'having a hand job'. 'Fingering' or 'having a feel' is when a girl has her vagina or sex passage and sometimes her clitoris stroked and rubbed. This can be very pleasant. It can also be very nasty. If your partner cares for you and is trying to make you feel good as well as satisfy their own desires, then the experience can be all right. But if all that is going on is that one person wants to score points and boast to friends or to find out what it is like, then you may well end up feeling used and abused. You could also feel sore. Genitals are made of delicate skin that can be scratched very easily if your partner is rough. A dirty finger could also give you an infection.

A 'hand job' is when a boy's sex organs are rubbed by

someone else to give him pleasure. You, too, can be hurt if fingernails are ragged or your partner is too rough.

If you become sexually excited but don't have an orgasm – whether you excite yourself or someone else does it! – you may feel sore afterwards. This is because all those parts that swell up – your penis and scrotum if you are a boy, your breasts and the lips surrounding the sex passage if you are a girl – will go down or 'detumesce' quite naturally and quickly if you 'come'. But if you are left unsatisfied, they stay like that for some time and leave you feeling a bit bruised. Some boys call this having 'blue balls'. It's uncomfortable, but not at all dangerous. *Don't* let him talk you into having sex to save him from suffering!

Why do people pet? It seems a silly question, but with all the dreadful warnings you may hear about the dangers of sex and the awful things that can happen to you, you might wonder. Many adults talk about sex as something boys want to do *to* a girl. This leaves boys and girls unprepared for what they may feel at the time, which is that *both* may want to do it. Another strong urge is simple curiosity. If no-one has ever overcome their and your natural shyness about sex and answered your questions, you may decide that 'doing it' is the best way to learn. A further pressure is people's attitudes towards what is 'normal' in friendships at this age. Everyone seems to assume that it's 'normal' to have a boy- or girlfriend – and that all boy-girl friendships are necessarily sexual.

There is still a lot of pressure in our society for women to think they are failures if they haven't got a man. This trickles down, so that girls are led to believe that there is something wrong with them if they haven't caught themselves that essential accessory – a boyfriend. For boys, it's a bit different. They don't need a girlfriend – but they *do* have to prove their manhood by losing their virginity.

'Virgin' is the word we use to describe someone who has not had full intercourse or sex. It applies to boys as well as girls. Being a virgin is nothing to be ashamed or proud about – it just *is*. All of us start off as virgins and most of us stop being one at some point in our lives. Wise virgins, however, don't 'lose' or 'give away' their virginity or have it 'taken'. They share the passing of it in joy and happiness with someone they care for. And *that* applies to boys, too! Since the word does relate to full sex, you cannot 'lose your virginity' during petting, nor can a girl do so by using tampons.

Lots of boys and girls are really quite happy going places and sharing thoughts with others of their own sex at this age. But we all get caught in a vicious circle. Everyone – teenagers and adults alike – starts worrying about whether you are keeping up. It's thought that the right behaviour for this time of your life is having a special friend of the opposite sex. So you may start a relationship just to show you're o.k. And everyone tells stories about what they do with their boy- or girlfriend to prove there's nothing wrong – or 'queer' – about them! And you get into a spiral of doing what you think your friends are doing, because *they've* told *you* what *they* think *you're* doing! 90% of these boasts are probably exaggerated or downright dreams.

You may well have found a boy- or girlfriend whose company you enjoy. And you may well find that you like to hold hands, kiss and cuddle. But do you need, or want, to go further at the moment?

Adults can baffle you at this stage. They nag at you to be a 'real girl' or a 'real boy' and get a partner . . . and when you do, they spend their time giving you dreadful hints and having fits if they think you've been alone for 2 minutes! It can be easy to decide: 'I might as well jump into bed – I'm being treated as if I do already'!

They may also sneer at your strong feelings and call them 'puppy love'. The idea is that just because they think your love will not last a lifetime, it is somehow unimportant. But they are wrong. Teenage love is probably the strongest emotion you will ever feel and even if it does fade, that makes the feelings no less real. The most famous lovers in the world, who killed themselves rather than live without each other, were 13 and 15 years old. Their names were Juliet and Romeo!

Try not to let parents and other adults get to you. The

chances are that the adults who laugh are actually suffering from painful memories as they watch you. They probably think they will save you from pain if they can laugh you out of your feelings. Remind them that making fun probably didn't help *them* when they were young, either! And that the more they laugh, the less likely you are to go to them for help or sympathy.

The answer is not to let anyone or anything push you around, whether it's the direct pressure of your friends or the beliefs of adults. . . Don't be forced into doing something you don't want because you fear you are unusual or abnormal. If you masturbate, have sexy dreams, thoughts and feelings . . . you *are* normal. If you find the whole thing a bit uninteresting and would rather wait a few years . . . you *are* normal. NORMAL IS YOU! If you allow yourself to be talked into behaviour you find uncomfortable, you won't be normal. Just conned!

9. The Whole Way

'I went the whole way with Steve because I loved him and he loved me. It wasn't at all like I'd expected – I'd heard from friends that it would hurt or be fantastic. It wasn't really any of that. But it did mean something, and I was glad we did it' – Sue E.

There will probably come a time when you want to 'go all the way' with the person you love. Having sex is given many different words and descriptions. We call it 'sleeping with someone', 'making love', 'screwing', 'fucking' and many more. The words you choose may well indicate how you feel about the situation. 'Making love' is actually a very different thing from 'fucking', isn't it?

This chapter will tell you about making love and about avoiding a pregnancy if you don't want a baby. Knowing about these things is not the same as wanting to go off and do them immediately. Your parents taught you about road safety a long time before they expected you to cross roads on your own. In the same way, it is a good idea to know about an important part of your future life before you plan to put it into action. Having sex is not compulsory! It won't prove anything, to yourself or others. You don't owe sex to a boy, however nice he has been or however much he has spent on you. As a boy, you don't have to make love to a girl to prove you love her. If you have the slightest doubts about whether to make love or not, *wait* until you are sure.

There are 3 reasons why people have sex. You could say they are the 3 Rs – though very different ones from the Reading, Writing and 'Rithmetic of school! The 3 Rs of sex are Reproduction, Recreation and Relationship. In other words, making babies, having fun or showing love. At the right time, and with the right person, all these reasons are good ones. But part of being an adult is making sure that you and your partner share the same view of what you are doing! It is cruel and nasty to pretend, for instance, that you are making love when you are, in fact, just having fun. It is absolutely unforgivable to try for a pregnancy when your partner has made it clear that they want nothing of the sort.

Many people in our society believe that you should only make love within marriage. Such a belief has merits – as long as you stick to it. Adults who thunder against sex *before* but have affairs *after* marriage are hardly giving you a good example. Nor are people who keep to these rules but make everyone miserable. Which is worse: happy sex which hurts no-one outside marriage, or miserable sex which makes husbands, wives and kids unhappy inside marriage? Many adults also only pay 'lip service' to these ideas. This means that they say they believe in saving yourself for marriage but actually didn't. Sex before marriage isn't something your generation invented! It's been going on since marriages started, and there were unmarried mums, teenage pregnancies and shotgun marriages in your parents', grandparents' and great-grandparents' time.

Many people also apply the 'No sex before marriage' rule only to girls. Girls who break this rule are called 'slags', 'sluts', 'nymphos' and other cruel names. Boys, on the other hand, are 'just like his dad!' 'real men', 'Jack the lad', or 'just sowing his wild oats'. Hardly fair! Could this be because boys do not get pregnant?

You may not agree with your parents' view, but don't think that you can throw a lifetime's upbringing out of the window, because you can't. If you've been brought up to wait for marriage, think very carefully before you act otherwise. The unhappiness and guilt you may feel will not be worth a few minutes' pleasure. And if this *is* how you feel, you probably won't even enjoy it at the time. You can't keep a foot in both camps. If you think 'Good girls don't' and you want to remain one, then you can't allow yourself to be swept away by overwhelming passion; no-one will cheer when you get 'a little bit' pregnant. Good girls and boys *do* – but they're good because they admit honestly to themselves what is happening and do it right.

Doing it right means taking adult responsibility for your actions. It means hurting nobody; not your parents, your friends, your partner or yourself. It means making love for the one good reason and none of the bad ones. Bad reasons for making love can include:

'It will prove I love him/her.'
'It will show them I'm a real man/woman.'
'It will make me grown up.'
'It will give me a baby who will love me.'
'Everyone does it.'

None of these is valid. The one good reason is because this is the right person and the right time and you are *really* sure.

If you do feel that you want to show your feelings by more than kissing and caressing, what then?

There can be no rules about the Right Time to make love. It may come when you are 16 or 17, 26 or 27. It may be on a rainy night in Wigan or a moonlit evening in Spain. It might be with your first boyfriend or only with your husband – before or on the honeymoon. The only real rule to stick to is, if in doubt, DON'T.

Sex can be marvellous. What happens is that after kissing and caressing each other, both of you will feel excited and eager. The man's penis will become stiff and stand up. The woman's sex passage will become wet and slippery. Both of them will find it feels nice if his penis slides into her vagina and they move together. His penis and her clitoris – the tiny nub of flesh, hidden in the folds of skin in the front of her water passage – are rubbed gently by this in-and-out movement. If both partners are gentle, loving and equally aroused, they will both feel waves of pleasure which build up to an orgasm or climax. Sticky white liquid – semen or 'spunk' – will gush out of his penis as he 'comes'.

On the other hand, sex can be pretty awful. If you are in an uncomfortable place or frightened someone may come in and disturb you, neither of you will really enjoy it. A woman may not become excited: instead of being wet, her vagina will be dry.

WIGAN, MARCH 86

This will mean that his penis may hurt her as they try to make love. She is then quite likely to be unable to come to a climax. If he is nervous, he may well lose his erection or 'come' too soon, before either of them has enjoyed it. Because you do feel so vulnerable when you are in love, an embarrassing or painful experience could well mark you for years. This is why it really *is* worth waiting and not rushing in too soon.

Sex can also be terrible if it's been forced on the girl by a selfish or over-eager boy. Forced sex is called 'rape'. Rape isn't just what happens when a 'sex maniac' jumps out of the bushes and drags a complete stranger off into a field. Rape is what happens when *any* man – whether it's your boyfriend, husband or a stranger – has sex with you when you didn't want to. Rape doesn't have to happen at knife-point, either. Threats and force take many forms. He's forcing you if he says he'll tell everyone you're a slag or a lesbian if you say 'no'; or that he *will* beat you up if you resist. Obviously you're being pretty unfair and silly if you lead on and excite a boy and then suddenly change your mind at the last moment. But, if you are going to say 'no', say it and mean it. If somebody does force you, *don't* believe them or anyone else if they say it was your fault or that you asked for it. Rape is a horrible crime committed by childish, stupid men. There are sensible, caring people who will help you if you're unlucky enough to have it happen to you.

Nothing spoils love as much as lying there afterwards thinking 'I wonder if I/she will get pregnant!' When the man comes, the teaspoon of fluid that gushes out of his penis contains about 300 *million* tiny sperm or seed. It only needs one of these to swim up her vagina, into her womb, up one of the fallopian tubes and to meet an egg – and she is pregnant.

Pregnancy is a bit like Russian roulette. There is only one egg a month, so you'd think the odds are against your being unlucky. But the egg takes a week to travel down the fallopian tube, and can be fertilized at any time in the first 3 days. Sperm also live for up to 3 days. Add to that the fact that ovulation – the release of an egg – can happen unexpectedly, and you see that you are actually at risk of pregnancy at any time! If you *do* risk it and are lucky, don't assume that your luck will hold. It won't.

Whether you and your partner talk about birth control before you make love and whether you use it is one of the best tests of a good relationship. Because if you're too shy to discuss it, too shy to use it or feel that it will spoil lovemaking, then this fact is very clear: one or both of you is too young, too silly or too selfish to even be thinking of having a sexual relationship. Or you just don't know each other well enough.

Sex is for people who love each other. Which means they care about whether their partner will be made unhappy by an unwanted pregnancy or too early responsibility.

Sex is for adults. Which means they overcome shyness and ask for birth control from a chemist or doctor. They accept a little inconvenience to avoid greater misery.

Sex leads to strong feelings and pregnancy. Which means you only have it with someone you want to care for you and you don't believe silly lies that say: 'You can't get pregnant the first time . . . if you do it standing up . . . if he's "careful" . . . if she doesn't enjoy it.'

Sex is for friends. Which means you should be able to share all your fears and feelings without embarrassment.

If just *one* of these reasons for not doing it rings a bell, then say no and wait. And this applies to males as well as females! But if this *is* the right time, the right partner and you have the right place waiting – what then? Before you rush off to celebrate your love, you will need to decide whether you would both like a baby to be a result of it. If not, read chapter 6 again – and act on it!

10. Someone Your Own Sex ·

'**M**y Dad used to make jokes about a bloke in his factory – he called him "Queenie" and was always going on about "that filthy poofter". He'd tell me to watch out for people like that. How could I tell him that I was becoming "someone like that" myself? I spent years of misery and even tried to kill myself because he made me so ashamed and sick with guilt at my own feelings' – Gary S.

Love makes the world go round, they say. And looking at films, reading books or magazines or listening to songs, you'd think that the only important thing in life is finding someone to love. Yet our society does seem to have some pretty strict rules about who you can and cannot love. The strictest is against loving someone your own sex.

Having a romantic or sexual feeling for the opposite sex is called being heterosexual – and this is seen as 'normal'. If you prefer a fellow boy or girl, you are a homosexual, which means 'same sex'. Being homosexual is felt by many to be 'abnormal'. When faced with something mysterious and frightening, people often invent slang terms which are supposed to be hurtful and nasty. 'Poofter', 'poof', 'queer', 'queen', 'fag', 'faggot', 'fairy' or 'pansy' are all words used to describe a male homosexual. Women homosexuals, or lesbians, are often called 'lezzies' or 'dykes'. Homosexuals themselves started using the word 'gay' as a reaction to these terms, to show that they had nothing to be ashamed of in their feelings. Gays can sometimes appear to push the idea of 'gay love' as being o.k. and be quite loud about their attitudes. This is hardly surprising. If you spent your whole life being told how wrong and odd you were, you might decide the only way to keep sane was to shout back!

Homosexual love hasn't always been forbidden. We have plenty of evidence to show that such love was an accepted part

τᾶς κε βολλοίμαν ἔρατόν τε βᾶμα
κἀμάρυχμα λάμπρον ἴδην
προσώπω
ἢ τὰ Λύδων ἄρματα καὶ
πανόπλοις
πεσδομάχευτας
LESBOS
Eressos
Mitilini
N
ÆGEAN SEA
I
RATHER
WALK
BRIGHT
HER
THE
AND
WOULD
SEE HER LOVELY
AND THE
RADIANCE OF
FACE THAN
LYDIAN CHARIOTS
ARMED INFANTRY
SAPPHO
POET born 600 bc, LESBOS, GREECE.

of life in many cultures. In ancient Greece, for instance, it was only frowned upon if an older man was unfairly using age and experience to seduce a youngster. In fact, the word 'lesbian' was coined by the Victorians after a famous poet of ancient times who lived on the island of Lesbos and wrote love songs to her

friends. Many other cultures saw, and still see, feelings and showing love as a way of worshipping God and celebrating the joys of life and don't get so het up as we do about who does what to whom! In our culture, love and sex are seen as wrong and wicked unless they lead to the logical end – pregnancy and a baby. Therefore, homosexual love, because it is obviously 'barren' and will never result in a child, is seen as unnatural.

Nowadays it is no longer a crime to be homosexual, but if you are a man you have to be over 21 and only show your feelings in private. Even so, life can be made very difficult and unpleasant for homosexual men and women. Many find they are refused jobs, especially if they want to work with young people as teachers or youth workers, or in 'security' work such as the Armed Forces, the Police or the Civil Service. Even worse, many gays are bullied and beaten up and almost have to accept this as a part of life.

The fact that so many people find these feelings strange, alarming and even unpleasant means that few people talk openly about being gay. Instead, it is talked about in hints and jokes. Rather than understanding homosexuals as people, they are seen as 'stereotypes'. This means we have one fixed picture about what we think a gay man or woman is like. It is imagined that all gay men want to imitate women and that all gay women copy men. The 'stereotype' picture of a gay man is that he must be limp-wristed, pretty, have styled hair, wear feminine clothes and mince about talking in a high voice. A lesbian is expected to thump about in boots and dungarees and smoke roll-ups or even a pipe. Some gays *do* do this – almost as a joke against 'straights' or heterosexuals but the sexual preferences of most gays *cannot* be seen just by looking at them. Some of the most 'macho' men and feminine women you could hope to meet are gay. In fact, you'd be surprised how many pop and film stars prefer their own sex!

All of us go through a period in our lives when we are attracted to people of our own sex. This is part of the complicated changes our bodies and emotions pass through on the journey from being a child to being an adult. Your body matures and becomes more able to respond sexually as it becomes capable of starting a pregnancy. At the same time, you become able to feel an emotional attachment different from the love you feel for your parents or other relatives or friends. Crushes and infatuations with actors and pop stars are part of 'practising' these emotions for a real person. So is falling for an older person you know, someone you like and admire such as a teacher or a prefect or a friend's brother or sister. Sometimes it is a close friend of your own age. In all these cases, it is usually a person of your own sex. After all, at this age, you have a lot more in common with them than the opposite sex. *Very* few people never have such feelings. Those who say they don't are usually not telling the truth.

But what happens at the end of this period? Being a homosexual is a bit like being left-handed. Most babies and toddlers go through a period of using both hands equally. Eventually, most settle on being right-handed. This does not mean that the ones who stay able to use both hands equally, or are left-handed, are wrong or childish or unnatural. That is just the way they are. So it is with sexual preferences. The best way of picturing it is to imagine a line of 100 people. 5 at one end will never experience any attraction to their own sex. 5 at the other end will *only* feel such love. The other 90 are strung out along that line. Those in the middle happily have relationships with both sexes. Some are mainly homosexual but can have sex with the opposite sex. Some are mainly heterosexual but are able and willing to have a homosexual relationship at some times. Lots of people, for instance, strike up such a friendship at an all-boy or girl boarding school, or on holiday, or in prison or during wars. Experimenting with friends during your teenage years – or at any other time – does not make you a homosexual for good. Homosexuality is not a disease you can catch, either by having sex with or feeling affection for someone your own sex or by spending time with them. Many people fear this, which is why gays will be hounded out of jobs or even their homes because straights are terrified of 'catching' their sexual preferences. Many good friendships are spoiled because one of the friends becomes afraid of strong but natural feelings of affection and stops the relationship. This fear also leads to the belief that gays are dangerous to children. People who believe this are often rather confused as to why they think so. On the one hand, it is said that many gays want to attack or seduce children. In fact, a sexual attraction for children – called paedophilia – is something very different from a liking for your own sex. Gays are no more likely to be attracted to children than are straight men and women. On the other hand, the danger to children may be justified by saying gays will obviously want to make more of their own kind by corruption and seduction, since they cannot have gay children any other way.

This assumes that everyone wants to bring a copy of themselves into the world – which is not true of most straight men and women. It also ignores the fact that gays can, and often *do*, have children – you don't have to be in love to get a girl pregnant or become pregnant. Not all gays 'come out' – that is, declare to themselves and those around them that they are gay. Many are quite rightly frightened of what may happen to them and so keep it a dreadful secret all their lives. They may marry and have children, trying to persuade themselves and others that they are 'normal'.

Much of this unfair and cruel prejudice arises from the fact that most of us *are* bisexual, however slightly. In other words, we *can* feel affection and make love with people of both sexes. So people who found themselves attracted to a person of their own sex but were convinced such feelings were wicked, would accuse him or her of 'corrupting' them and turning their feelings from 'natural' heterosexual to 'unnatural' homosexual love. It is possible that people who go 'queer bashing' or who are most vicious and angry against homosexuality are actually trying to shout down their own feelings because they feel guilty about them.

Many people find homosexuality frightening and strange because their minds boggle at what gay couples might do to each other when they actually make love. When you think about it, most of making love is the same whether it happens between a man and a woman, or two men or two women. That is, most of it

is two people showing their feelings of love and attraction by kissing and caressing each other. When it is a man and a woman, part – but actually only part – of this is sexual inter-course, when the man's penis is put in the woman's vagina. With two men, or two women, as much physical satisfaction is felt by 'mutual masturbation': that is, when both caress their bodies and rub each other's sexual organs until they have an orgasm. Some gay men also have intercourse by using the back passage or rectum in place of the vagina. This is pleasurable for both. The 'passive' man who receives his partner's penis feels pleasure since the anus or entry to the back passage has nerve endings which react to the in-and-out movement. If you think about it, you feel a similar pleasure when you pass a motion on the lavatory. Also, the passive man will feel excitement as a gland called the prostrate is rubbed by the pressure of his lover's penis through the walls of the rectum. This can bring on an orgasm. The 'active' lover, of course, feels the same pleasure a straight man has in sexual intercourse.

In most societies, the waste matter we expel from our bodies is thought to be dirty. Even heterosexual sex is seen by many to be nasty because our sex organs are placed so near to our 'excretory' or waste organs. 'Sodomy' or anal sex gives male homosexual love an even dirtier image. And anal intercourse is against the law, whatever your age. It's even illegal between a married couple!

Yet most gay love is actually a matter of mutual caresses and kisses, not intercourse. But most people can only think of sexual love in terms of one person putting a part of their body inside the other person, and assume this occurs in all gay affairs. It doesn't.

It is as difficult to say why a particular person is gay as it would be to work out why a particular person goes for tall blonds or chunky redheads. We are sure now that it has nothing obviously to do with our physical make-up. It used to be believed that men with extra female hormones, or women with extra male hormones, became gay. Men who were frail or women who were strong were labelled as homosexual. Women are still terrified of taking up a sport in case they build up muscles and start looking 'athletic'. For 'athletic', read 'queer'! It is more likely to be your early childhood experiences which lead you to find your own sex more attractive than the opposite sex. But the reasons are complicated and can often be hard to pinpoint. Some parents and authorities try to protect a child against homosexual influences by removing it from a parent who is gay. This is silly. Since straight parents have gay children, it is quite obvious that sexual tastes are not simply copied from our parents. Children have been brought up through the ages by gay parents – both those who were open and those who hid their feelings – and there is no proof that it is 'passed on'.

If you think you might be gay, what should you do? If you are still a teenager, it might be best to wait a few years before labelling yourself 'gay'. Labels have a way of sticking. Leave your options open and you can make a free choice when you are ready.

It is best to give yourself a few years to make sure this is really how you are rather than the feelings all teenagers pass through. In the same way, you'd be a fool if you decided that you were only attracted to tall, green-eyed redheads at 16 and passed up all the medium-sized blonds and dark-haired people you might like at 19. Quite apart from anything else, if you are male, homosexuality is illegal before you are 21. If you are both young, someone could make it unpleasant and embarrassing for you. If your lover is over 21, he can really be in trouble. Curiously, *female* homosexuality is not against the law. The story is that when Queen Victoria signed the Sexual Offences Act, she refused to believe that women could do such a thing!

It could help to talk to someone about this. You could go to a Youth Advisory Centre and see people who are used to dealing with all sorts of problems. They won't be shocked or disgusted – or surprised! – at what you are feeling. You could also talk to people who *are* gay, such as 'Gay Switchboard' or 'Friend'. They won't try to persuade you to 'come over', but will help you sort yourself out, whichever way!

If you know someone who is gay, what should you do? For a start, don't jump to conclusions. Just because a friend is affectionate or a 'toucher' doesn't mean to say that they are gay. Putting an arm around you, patting or touching you, grabbing your hand, kissing you on the cheek, looking at you in the shower or just wanting to be alone with you is not proof of any sexual interest. Many western cultures are a shy and stiff-upper-lip lot and can be surprised and embarrassed at what many other people consider normal and friendly behaviour. Your friend may come from a family where open and easy affection is accepted and encouraged. But, if you are right, what then? Don't flatter yourself that your friend is necessarily wanting to get off with you. Gay people, just like straight people, don't want an affair with everyone they know – and you may not be their type.

But what if you are made an offer? You are not going to be changed or tainted by their interest. If you are not interested, just say so.

If you *are* interested, the ground rules are the same as for any kind of sexual relationship. Be sure this is the right person and the right time. Be sure that neither of you is going to be hurt, abused or used. Be sure that neither your own or anyone else's feelings of guilt or regret are going to make you unhappy. And if in the slightest doubt, DON'T.

However, if the offer comes from someone much older than you, that is a very different matter. As with a heterosexual affair, an age gap of 10 years or so should make you very wary. Someone your own age has the same needs and can be hurt as much as you. It's a bit like a game – you both have the same stake, the same cards and as much to win or lose. But an older person has far more power – and you could find yourself in a game where you don't know the rules. Don't be flattered or overawed by their interest.

If you find you have gay friends, try not to judge their whole lives and personalities by what they like to do in bed. You don't refuse to be friends or respect people because they like redheads and you like blonds, do you? And you don't refuse to go to the disco with someone because you love swimming and they hate water? Sexual likes and dislikes are a very small part of everyone's lives. There are other, far more important, parts that you can share and enjoy. One advantage of having a gay friend of the opposite sex is that you can really relax without having to worry about whether one of you is going to, or should be, making a pass. The advantage of a gay friend of your own sex is that you'll never be rivals for someone you fancy!

11. Marriage And Parenthood

'll get married and have children, I suppose. I mean, everyone does, don't they? Having a place of my own would be nice, and a kid who loves you and looks up to you. Still, you don't really have to *marry* to get all that these days. Marriage is a bit out of date, isn't it?' – Yvonne P.

Which do you think is the main point of marriage – the white dress and the fuss everyone makes of the bride and groom? Or the promise they make to each other? If you think the private promise, to love and look after each other, is the more important, then you can see that "marriage" has been with us since before human beings came down from the trees. And even some animals "marry" or mate for life. Swans choose one partner and stay together. If one of them dies, the other will sometimes die from sadness. A Christian ceremony in church is only one of the *many* ways a couple can promise to be a partnership for ever. Marriage can mean as much – or as little – to a couple if it's celebrated in a cathedral in front of hundreds of people or in a Registry Office with two friends. Some couples can stay faithfully together all their lives without going through a formal ceremony, while others cheat on each other almost as soon as the honeymoon is over!

So, while the *wedding* can be important as a way of saying: "Look, everybody, we're serious about this", it is the *commitment*, or promise you give to each other, that makes a marriage.

Most people will get married at some point in their lives. This isn't to say that if you don't there is something wrong with you. Sadly, a lot of people use the word for an unmarried woman – a 'spinster' – to mean a dried-up old maid, a failure. And 'elderly bachelor' is often said with a nudge and a wink to show you'd just as happily say 'queer'. Young people leap into marriage with the wrong person, at the wrong time or for the wrong reasons, to avoid being called these names.

Which is a pity, because marriage can be wonderful. But it can also be terrible. 1 in 4 couples end their marriage in divorce, and nobody knows how many just go their separate ways, or how many put up with a 'shell marriage'. This is when the outside or shell, of the marriage seems happy and normal but, inside, there is bitterness or a simple lack of caring. There are good and bad reasons for getting married. As with deciding to have sex, there is really only one good reason! Which is that you have found the right person at the right time in your life!

Being in love is often not enough. Some marry because 'I can't live without you'. But you also need to know you can live *with* your chosen partner. It's not always the same thing! You need to be mature enough to cope with setting up home with another adult. It's a different relationship to living with parents or family. There has to be give and take on both sides. If neither of you is prepared to listen to the other's needs and feelings, then you won't get on. If one of you is willing to be a 'doormat', you will still be heading for problems. Doormats come to resent being pushed around. Bullies just never grow up and get fed up too. The best way of working out if you *are* ready is to check that you are not marrying for any of the *bad* reasons. These can be because

'I want to get away from home.'

You might see marriage as an escape from your parents' rules. You'll be forgetting that the boring things your parents make you do at home will multiply in one of your own. Get married, and the two of you will not only have to keep your room but a whole flat or house tidy! *And* plan, buy and cook meals for yourselves, as well as loads of other chores. Yes, you can go out when you like . . . but the responsibility for another person's feelings will take the place of your parents' rules. Marriage is not a way of getting *away* from an old life. It's a step *into* a new life. Do it simply to escape and you will probably take all your misery *with* you.

'If I'm married, they'll have to see that I'm really grown up.'

Because most adults get married, we think the reverse is therefore true, that being married makes you, or shows that you are, adult. What a sad mistake! Certainly you can learn from the experience of marriage, and it can be one of the many things that helps you grow up. But, like water off a duck's back, some people can go through years of marriage and emerge as selfish and immature as they were on the first day. It's true that quite a lot of people will congratulate and welcome you when you marry, as if you had joined a club. But if marriage to you is just a game – a slightly older version of 'Mummies and Daddies' – you can bet that their pleasure will soon turn to scorn.

'I don't want to be left behind. All my friends are getting married.'
This can make life hard. Birds of a feather flock together – married couples usually drop their single friends. So, if all your friends are hitched, you may be on your own. But is this really a reason to take such a very serious step? And what if most of your friends get divorced, will you copy?

'It will show I'm not a failure or "queer".'
It is sad that women are still made to feel that the only mark of success is getting a husband. And men that they *must* prove masculinity through marriage. Both men and women can be perfectly happy having a busy, satisfying job and lots of friends. If you choose an empty marriage instead, you might end up feeling a worse failure.

'I need someone to look after me.'
Quite a few men marry because they want their shirts washed. And many women because they want their bills paid. Both of them are looking for a Mummy or Daddy to go on providing home comforts. This is fair enough – as long as you take care never to grow up and want a more adult relationship. And as long as Big Daddy or Mummy is happy to keep you.

You could satisfy any of these needs without making such a solemn promise as "til death us do part' and dragging someone else's dreams into it. Marriage should be left for when you both are really ready. Being part of a happy couple is probably the best thing that could ever happen to you. Making compromises and fitting into the other person's needs and likes becomes a pleasure. Because you *both* make allowances and *both* care as much, or more, about your partner's happiness and comfort as your own.

Choosing the person you want to share your life with should take a bit more thought than picking a new pair of shoes. Living with someone is going to affect what you do every day. It's also going to affect the course of your life – where you live, who your friends are and even what sort of job you have. Before you take the plunge, it might be an idea to discuss your views on such things as: marriage and being faithful, work, social life and having children.

It's a bit late, after the marriage, to find *he* thinks married women should stay home and have babies, while *she* wants a career and one child at 30. The problem with marriage for the wrong reasons is that so many people suffer for it. You, your partner, both your families . . . and any children. Because children do tend to appear in marriages, and not just happy ones.

If marriage has seemed to you to be the answer to all your problems, the chances are that having children has also looked rosy. In fact, many people – young people especially – who want to get married for the *wrong* reasons, force the issue with a pregnancy. These used to be called 'shotgun marriages'. The girl's angry father would use a 'little persuasion' to escort the offending boy to the altar to marry his daughter. Nowadays, fewer teenagers make this choice. Girls refuse because the 'stigma' or bad reputation of being an unmarried mum is less than it was in your parents' day. Both boys and girls realize that a forced marriage can be miserable. But every year some still do it. If you marry while still in your teens, or with a baby on the way, your marriage is 2 or 3 times more likely to fail than if you'd waited until your 20s and used birth control!

Children can set the seal on a happy marriage. They can give their parents joy, and be a lasting 'bond' or tie between them. But if you have a child to keep a shaky marriage together, or force your partner into the situation at all, the chances are the opposite will happen. Many people have children for all the advantages they *think* a baby can bring them. Such as:

MAKE SURE YOU ARE GETTING MARRIED FOR THE RIGHT REASONS

Love – a child will naturally adore you.

Status – everyone else will look up to you as a 'Mother' or 'Father'.

Power – a child will do as you say, instead of your being the one pushed around.

Proof of your sexuality – only 'real' men or women can start a baby.

Interest – it's less boring than hanging around on the Dole.

The problem is that it's not quite as simple as that. Looking at the television ads or listening to some people, you'd think that being a parent is one long round of sunshine and daisies. A child will smile and gurgle at you, the whole world will love you. Have a baby, and you and your loving partner will live in a dream house in bliss for ever.

These dreams we have about parenthood skate over the full facts. As well as smiling, babies also cry and scream. They wet nappies, and they may refuse the bottle or breast you offer them.

A baby has a mind of its own and he or she is not a toy or a doll which will do exactly as you want. Babies are physically *unable* to control their bowels and bladders until they are over 15 months old. A baby will only begin to understand simple instructions after 9 months or a year, and will not speak sentences before 2 years or more. And only then if *you* patiently and lovingly help them to learn. Babies and children are hard work. They are not selfish, but utterly helpless. Which means they need far more *from* you than they will be able to *give* you. If you become a parent when you and your partner understand and are prepared for all this, having children can be a marvellous experience. Your pleasure will come from being able to watch and help in the development of a tiny scrap that comes from both your bodies. But, start a child when it is *you* who needs love and care, and you may well find it all too much.

Some people decide having children is not for them. Such a choice is becoming less unusual and is certainly not 'abnormal'. Having children will change your life and your relationship. After all, living with 2 or more people has got to be different to living with 1! For some, the joy they might have in being a parent does not make up for losing the close, one-to-one relationship a 'childfree' marriage will allow. *When* and *if* you have children should be left to your personal choice. It's far too important to drift into because 'everyone else does it' or 'my mother wants grandsons'. Most mistakes in life can be put behind you. A bad sexual experience can be forgotten. An unhappy marriage can be finished. But, once a baby is born, he or she is in this world for life. You'd want to make sure this only happens when everyone concerned is ready to make that life a happy one, wouldn't you?

12. Our Customs And The Way We Live

'I don't go to church, so I'd say that religion has no part in my life. But, when I think about it, some of my friends have very different rules about the way they live, and they come from different religions. So I suppose, even if you don't believe in it, your family's religion must change the way you look at things' – Carole T.

Religious beliefs and practices were once a very important part of everyone's life. Village society used to revolve around the church and religious festivals. Nowadays, organized religion seems to have less meaning for most people. But this does not mean that religion doesn't affect your life, in the most surprising ways. The point is that your "culture" and your religion are very firmly linked. Your culture is the way of life you share with the people you were brought up with. Religious rules become the basic foundation of a culture. You may decide not to accept that religion, but you will still find yourself taking these rules for granted, without realizing where they come from. All religions share certain obvious ones such as not stealing or killing. But each culture also has its own particular regulations. If you have friends or come up against people who are from a different culture, you may end up hurting their feelings if you don't understand why you and they can be playing to a different set of rules.

For instance, you may have schoolfriends whose parents came originally from North Africa, the Middle East, Afghanistan or Pakistan. You might have thought it a good laugh to tease the boys during swimming classes because they wore long trunks, or to complain to the gym mistress because the girls were allowed off. They might have found it difficult to defend themselves from your teasing, since they may not share their parents' strict views. But their parents may well be followers of the Muslim religion, also called Islam. Muslim men must cover their bodies from knee to navel (or belly button) at all times. Women must not reveal the shape of their bodies at all. Strict Muslim women hide everything except face and hands – and some even wear a face mask!

A friend whose parents come from the Punjab – the North West of India – might be a Sikh. Boys must not cut their hair, and wear it in a topknot under a handkerchief. When they reach adulthood, their long hair is tied up in a turban. Muslims and Sikhs are both forbidden to drink any alcohol at all. You might think it exciting to go into a pub or to drink at home when your parents are out – half the fun is in knowing that this is forbidden when you are young. For some of you, however, the excitement is outweighed by the guilt you would feel at going against your parents. You can be pulled between what your friends are urging you to do and what you know your parents would say. For a Sikh or Muslim teenager, the battle can be far worse. They know they will be breaking a very important rule if they have a drink. For a Westerner, drinking at 16 is just a question of jumping the gun. For a Sikh or Muslim, it's breaking a life-long rule. You would be very cruel or stupid to tease such a friend for being childish or afraid by saying no.

Hinduism is found among people coming originally from India. Young people are taught to have a very strong respect for the older men in the family. You may have a Hindu friend who is noisy and pushy with you and your friends, but see him at home in front of his father or elder brother and he would be a different person. He wouldn't interrupt them and wouldn't even smoke a cigarette in their sight, since this would be showing disrespect! Hindu and Muslim girls have a very strict upbringing. Hindu parents nearly always choose their daughters' husbands. Most Muslim parents do this too. This means that girls are not allowed to have boyfriends or even go to discos or parties. Such girls may seem to be unfriendly or standoffish. You can hardly blame them. If a brother, sister or cousin reports even an innocent talk with a boy, the girl can be punished by her parents. Sikh girls have more freedom, but since they must marry inside the faith, they too may seem less friendly than you consider normal.

Most non-Christian religions have rules about food, so if you have a friend home for tea, it's a good idea to check first what they will be able to eat. Jews and Muslims are not allowed to eat pork, so bacon butties are out. Jews are also forbidden to mix "meat and dairy" – so cheeseburgers would be a no-no. Muslims, Sikhs and Jews must only eat meat that has been butchered in a certain way, so you might be better off offering beans on toast.

Many religious rules have a very sensible reason behind them. The rules about food, for instance, came about because in the old days before modern farming methods pork carried dangerous parasites that could harm us. Meat would go bad very quickly unless it was drained of blood during butchering. Modern cooking and refrigeration makes these laws unnecessary, but they still hang on because most people have forgotten why they were invented.

Another "hangover" is the rules about sex. Most of our rules about friendships between the sexes date back to the days when women were not considered as people in their own right. Women could not own land or property or make their own choices in life. They existed to breed sons. The most important thing a man could have was a son to carry on his name and inherit his property. However, the only way he could be sure that his wife's son was *his* was to insist that she was a virgin at marriage and remained faithful afterwards. In many religions and cultures, these laws still exist. In Western culture, the *laws* have changed. Women can have jobs, own property and choose whom they marry. But, in our heart of hearts, many of us still accept social rules that echo the old laws. In spite of the fact that a woman's role in life is no longer just to breed sons for her husband, *we* still feel that women should be virgin brides. But men can have as much experience as they want.

One way of trying to keep to the rule of not having sex before marriage is to do it – but pretend we aren't. So, "getting carried away" every Saturday night with your boyfriend is o.k. Marching along to the birth control clinic and getting contraception is not. You might make excuses that using birth control "spoils it" or that 'it makes it unromantic and cold to plan it", but you'd be fooling yourself. What you are really doing is reacting to the religious teaching that tells you that sex is a nasty, dirty and embarrassing activity . . . that you should save for marriage. As long as you don't *admit* that you are having sex, you can pretend that you are still a "nice girl" or a "pure boy".

As with any of these cultural, religious rules, it is plain good manners and sense to find out what your friends think is right. If someone you know wears clothes or has a hairstyle you think is odd, why not ask them about it instead of teasing them? If the food they eat is different, why not try it yourself and find out why? And if they seem shy or unfriendly, why not try to understand why this might be, rather than blaming them? However unreasonable or silly you think their behaviour, it's certain that you and your friends do things just as foolish for similar reasons. The trick is to find out what the rules are, and to make sure you all fit in with each other.

13. My Parents Don't Understand Me!

'**S**ometimes, I really feel as if I hate my parents. They don't try to listen or understand and they still treat me as if I was 4 years old' – Theresa M.
'Theresa used to be such a good child – thoughtful, kind. Now, she's rude and selfish and I just don't know what's happened!' – Theresa's Mum.

Puberty may have brought you a new body, periods or wet dreams and all sorts of frightening and exciting changes. But it has also brought you a new relationship with your parents. And, if you are the average teenager, that relationship could be full of quarrels and misunderstandings.

But, however much you may seem at loggerheads, it *is* possible for you to get on with your parents. It just takes a little understanding, a little compromise and a little effort. It would be worth it, so how do you go about it?

For a start, you should realize that *all* teenagers have difficulties with their parents. You are not specially disobedient and they are not specially strict or unfair, whatever any of you thinks! So, if we all share these difficulties, why do they arise? Maybe, if you could understand the causes, it would help you to do something about them.

You must remember that your parents have watched you grow over the years. Because they were adults when you were born, they have a perfect memory of you as a little child. You may have forgotten that time – you look in a mirror now and see a face and body that are almost adult and cannot understand *why* they still treat you as a baby. After all, if you are 16, being an 8-year-old is half a lifetime away. But look at it from your parents' point of view. If they are in their late 30s or 40s, you were a child less than a fifth of *their* lifetime ago. So when they look at

FATHERS FIND IT HARD TO ACCEPT THAT THEIR LITTLE GIRL IS GROWING UP

you, they can still see and hear the person you were. It's almost as if they were looking at one of those trick photographs with two images combined. You see the adult, they see the child. Fathers find it hard to accept that "their little girl" (or mothers that "their little boy") is growing up and that they no longer come first in your affections. All girls practise their developing skills of flirting and using their sexual attraction on the men they see every day, such as relatives. Your father may respond to this because he can see your mother – his wife – young and beautiful again in you. Hardly surprising that he may react with fear and jealousy at any hint that you may be growing up and wanting to shift your attention to another man. And a spotty youth who won't respect or care for you, at that! It's exactly the same for mothers.

Your mother has her own troubles at this time. It is quite likely that as you approach the most attractive and sexual stage in your life, she is coming to an important end point. Women go through the "menopause" at any time from the middle to the late 40s. This means that their periods stop and they can no longer become pregnant. The body changes that stop their periods can also bring other symptoms – sudden waves of sweating, dizziness, depression and fear. Of course, your mother is hardly likely to want to have another baby, and the end of being able to get pregnant does *not* mean she can no longer have and enjoy sex. But, in our society, we tend to think that sex is only for the young and beautiful and that a woman is only *truly* a woman if she can get pregnant. So your poor Mum may be struggling with her feelings about being old and no longer attractive *just* at the time when you are discovering your pleasure in a new and attractive body and in sexual possibilities. That's a certain recipe for envy and anger. And your father may have his own struggle with a spreading waistline and receding hair. His little boy, who used to look up to him, becomes a rival to be put firmly in place.

And what of your feelings? You may not realize it, but at this age you are practising how to stand on your own two feet. You are finding that you no longer accept that "mother knows best". You want to work out for yourself what to think and believe. You also want to take responsibility for your own actions and not to have to ask for permission to do things and go to places. This is why you find yourself reacting so angrily when your parents ask you: "When will you be home?" or "Who are you going to see?" Like anybody who is still raw and uncertain, you feel specially touchy when your skills are questioned. If you thought about it calmly, you would realize that some of the questions are quite reasonable. After all, Mum needs to know when you are going to be in so she can plan how many to feed at dinner, or when to lock up for the night. And Dad is being quite sensible, not babying you, if he is frightened of your walking home across a park at night, what with today's muggers, gangs and rapists.

So the skill you should perfect is how to recognize which are the reasonable questions and which are the ones they ask because they still want you to be a child. You need to learn how to control your objections to the first type and how to have an adult discussion with them over the second kind.

Human beings quarrel when they do not understand or care about the other person's point of view. This often shows itself in a "closed" question – a question which has no real answer because the person has already made up their mind. When you come into the kitchen, ready to go out, and your mother says: "You're not going out like that?", she's not asking you a question – she's telling you that she thinks you look awful. It's hardly surprising that you react defensively. But you probably do the same thing to her: "My mate gets £10 a week. It's not fair that you only give me £2!", invites the same sort of angry defence and a boring lecture from Dad on how hard up he is. So the trick is to try and spot the closed questions – both yours and theirs – and open them up.

Next time they ask you a "closed" question, take a deep breath before you shout, and think about it. Work out what they are *really* saying. For instance, "Do you mean you are worried about what people think of my clothes, Mum? But it's the fashion now, lots of people my age dress like this and we don't think it's odd. When you were a teenager, I bet your Mum said the same things about your clothes. What exactly do you dislike about them?" She may be so surprised she tells you not to be cheeky. But she is much more likely to sit down and talk to you about what she *really* fears. Strong reactions to how you look often come from a fear that you might give the wrong "signals" to people. I'm sure you've read of rape cases where the man said he thought the girl was willing because she was wearing a tight T-shirt or a short skirt. Or where boys have been beaten up because someone didn't like the way they dressed. But maybe you can explain that the signs of being "easy" or "odd" in her day were different. So many boys and girls wear these clothes now that most people realize that it isn't an open invitation or a sign you're strange. But think also about what she says, she may have a point!

When *you* have a question, try to put it in an open way. For instance, if you want an increase in pocket money, or to stay out late for a party, here's how you could approach them. Rather than demanding, threatening or attempting to blackmail your parents into agreeing by claiming all your friends are doing it, go to them with a list of thought-out reasons for the change and ask for a talk. Explain *why* you make your request and how you mean to do it. For example, "Mum, could we talk about my pocket money? You see, I'm finding it difficult to manage on £2 a week. Could I make a suggestion? Some of my friends get more money and have to buy their own clothes. I'd really like to have a go at managing my own money – practice for when I leave home. Could we work out what you usually give me for fares and things and then let me have that to budget for myself?" or "Mum, I'd like to go to my mate's party. It will end after midnight and I'd really feel stupid and miss out if I had to leave early. I know you'd worry, so could we work something out? I could arrange for a lift home, a taxi maybe. Or, if Dad would agree, he could be waiting outside at 12.15. If I'm not out by 12.30, he can come in and fetch me, but please could he wait in the car till then?'

By offering a compromise, you show you are willing to listen to their fears and not rush off all at once into being an adult. They won't feel left behind, but will trust you and be happy to let you go gradually. If you try to grab your freedom too quickly, they will try all the harder to hold you back. And if you *do* make a mistake, they will see it as proof that they were right, you *are* still a child and need to be looked after.

You may remember from English lessons that Shakespeare talked about "The seven ages of man". We tend, in our society, to see only two stages: child and adult. Children are powerless – they are looked after and told what to do. Adults have power – they can make their own decisions in life. We all want to rush into adulthood so that we can enjoy this power, and often miss the fact that taking responsibility needs practice first. You wouldn't expect to be made boss on your first day at work. We all have to go through a trainee or apprentice period. So, in fact, there are three stages to life. In the middle stage, called "adolescence", we are trainee adults, gradually learning the job.

Our parents can be nervous in this trainee period because they know the penalties for a mistake can be far worse than the penalties when you were learning to walk, or when you learn a job. A bruise or a botched piece of work don't matter very much, but a pregnancy, drug addiction or failure at exams leading to a dead-end job, will blight your whole life.

So, trust their love and concern for you while helping them to understand that you need to stand on your own feet and think for yourself, if you are to be a happy and fulfilled adult. If you are prepared to listen to them, they *will* listen to you.

Having said all this, it must be admitted that a few, very unlucky teenagers *do* have parents whose behaviour is unreasonable. Sometimes, you won't be able to manage to change things on your own and will need to ask for outside help.

For instance, there are parents who cannot, will not, allow their sons and daughters to grow up. In such an adult, care and concern for your well-being is twisted into an unnatural over-possessiveness. Against all reason and all the evidence, they insist the young people in their family are still "our little girl" or "just a lad". Instead of helping their children to grow and take responsibility for themselves, they try to keep them young and unable to cope on their own. There are other parents who find it difficult to show anger or worry with words and use fists instead. There are even some who warp the love between parent and child into sexual love.

There is a world of difference between the normal, healthy show of physical affection between relatives, and sexual attentions. Whether you are a boy or a girl, you should be able to share loving kisses and hugs with relatives and not be afraid or worried about it. You should be happy to walk hand in hand with your mother or father, exchange loving kisses or hug them. But *any* sort of touching of your sexual parts, any attempt by an older person to get you to touch their sexual parts, or any deep or "French" kissing, is not right. Just because you are young and under their authority, or they are bigger and stronger than you, does not mean you have to put up with *anything* that makes you miserable or hurts you.

Sexual contact with a relative is called incest. It's against the law, whether the other person is your parent, grandparent, uncle or aunt, brother or sister. The authorities, however, would be more interested in making sure you are saved from harm than in just locking up anyone who had been guilty of this crime. So if you and your brother or sister have fooled around and explored each other's bodies and neither of you have felt under any pressure from the other to do this, don't worry. You aren't going to be scarred for life or have the police on your trail! But, just as much, *don't* feel you have to put up with any unwelcome attentions. You can, and should, say "no". If no-one in your family will come to your aid or believe you when you tell them what happened, there are people who *will*.

Relatives or family friends who use their greater age and experience to push you around or handle you in this way are seldom "wicked". More likely, they too were treated badly when *they* were young. Punishment or jail may not be the best result for any of you. Depending, of course, on what happened and how you feel, the people who will help and protect you will be flexible. They may try to stop the person who ill-used you doing it again by getting them to understand why they acted like that.

Above all, you must realize that being beaten, kept in or sexually abused will never have been *your* fault. It won't have happened because *you* deserved it. It wasn't because *you* are a wicked person. It happened because the person who mistreated you had *their* problems. If anyone wants to point a finger or hand out blame, it should be to them, not you. The people who can help are your teachers, a youth club leader, a local social worker, your family doctor or priest, or any adult you trust. You could also go to any Youth Advisory Centre, either of the charities which help with incest (see the address list at the end of the book) or the NSPCC. The Samaritans and a Rape Crisis Centre would also help.

14. Getting On With Grown-Ups

'I used to live in terror of this bus conductor. He was really nasty to me one morning when I didn't have the right change and for years after I'd miss the bus if I saw he was on. I'd be late for school rather than face him' – Steve G.

When you're a child, you're likely to be treated quite well by the adults you meet. Even when you are being a noisy brat, strangers will smile and be kind to you. As you get nearer to being a teenager, this may change. You can probably think of quite a few adults you do not get on with. They may be people you only meet in passing – bus conductors, ticket collectors, shop assistants, policemen. Or they might be people with whom you have a closer acquaintance – teachers, neighbours and friends' parents.

Some adults treat teenagers as if you are a different species altogether, rather than just younger versions of themselves. Others act as if there was a war going on – them against you! The result can be unnecessary distrust and arguments. You can make life a lot easier for yourself if you try to understand *why* they behave in this way.

Teenagers get a "bad press": when young people are talked about in the papers or on television, everyone always seems to look at the bad side. Nobody wants to read about happy teenagers who get on with their friends and parents, do well at school and get through life with little fuss. That's boring. What they want to do is complain about punks, vandals, glue sniffers and unmarried mums. The result is that some adults see a crowd of teenagers and take it for granted that you have to be a gang of irresponsible hooligans on the rampage – even if you're actually on your way to the old people's home to help out!

You'd think that they would know better. Many of these

SOME ADULTS TREAT TEENAGERS AS A DIFFERENT SPECIES

adults have teenage children of their own – so don't they realize that you are not monsters? Of course, having teenagers can be the *reason* for their feeling hostile! Why is this? Well, young children and adults share one thing – they tend to accept things.

Children will do as they are told, and believe in Santa Claus, because Mummy says so and Mummy knows best. Adults will also take things for granted – because the boss says so, and that's how it's always done, or because otherwise "What would the neighbours think?" But teenagers are different. Adolescence is the time when you ask awkward questions. You want to find out for yourself rather than take their word for it. You want to form your own beliefs, rather than have them handed to you. How can you blame the adults around you for feeling uneasy and unhappy? Not only are you challenging ideas they feel are important – such as the existence of God – but, more important, you are questioning customs they *don't* really like but feel they must follow.

You may also set their teeth on edge because you have so much of your life in front of you. Even the most successful adult may feel that there were chances in life that they missed. For somebody in a dead-end job or with an unhappy private life, you represent all the possibilities they would like to have again. You might be worried stiff about unemployment or whether your friends really like you! At least you have another 50-60 years to make things better. The adult glaring at you may have only 10-20 years and he or she hasn't the benefit of youth to help them.

Probably the most important reason for some adults to be unpleasant to you is because, being young, you have less power than they do. A bus conductor may feel bitter because he has no control over his life. His boss pushes him around, his wife nags him and his children give him cheek. Then you offer a £5 note for a 20p fare and he can hit back. He may not have power with other people, but he has the authority to throw you off or be rude to you. Adults can push kids around and sneer at them in a way they would never dream of treating other adults. Why? Because other adults could shout back and maybe win the argument. Teenagers are perfect punching bags because they are often unable to hit back. If you are rude to a teacher, you can be punished. If a teacher is rude to you, that's all part of life.

So what can you do about it? For a start, try to understand

their point of view. If you and your friends gang up and make fun of someone, even an adult, you can't be surprised if they react against you. So, if only for self-protection, being rude or rowdy on buses is a bad idea. The next trip, you may be on your own! This doesn't mean that you have to behave like robots. But spare the conductor, and any other passengers, a nice smile or friendly comment. Ragging a teacher means that school just becomes a power game. Do you really want the point of a lesson to be who can come out on top? Or that you learn something that might be interesting and at least helps you pass exams?

Getting on with people is a skill that is worth practising and perfecting. One of the most important tricks is to look for what is *behind* an angry response or a sarcastic question. The shop assistant who won't serve you – is she tired or fed up? Did a group of teenagers steal from her yesterday? The teacher who sneers: "Don't you know that?" when you ask a question – does he envy your youth and want to crush your enthusiasm? Attacking these people won't make things better, only worse. Smart, cutting remarks will make them even more sure that teenagers are the enemy to be kept down. But, if you can go against what they expect and be calm and nice, you might get somewhere! Look people in the eye and think about what they have said. Then, answer them quietly. To the shop assistant say: "If you don't want to serve us all together, will it be alright if we go out and come back again one at a time?" For the teacher: "I'm sorry if I make you impatient, but surely it's better that I ask than get it wrong? I'm here to learn and I'd like your help."

Just as with your parents, you have to look for the "closed" questions and open them out. If someone stops you with: "And where do you think you're going?", you might be tempted to shout: "What's it to you?" or "Down here, what does it look like?" Both of these replies are just asking for a quarrel. What the person really meant was: "Hold on, I have a reason to want to stop you." The reason may be that he's in a bad mood and wants to stop your fun. Or that he's just spent 3 hours in laying a lawn you're about to trample. Or there's a hole in the road you're about to fall in! Wouldn't it be easier to open up his question and *ask* for his reason? 'Sorry, we're on our way to the bus/ disco/shops. Is there a problem?"

Maybe this would go against your pride. You resent these people having control over you and want to show them that you can do and say as you like. You have a straight choice. Keep your pride and go through your teenage years snarling and snapping at everyone who gets in your way. You may feel smart. You'll also have a hard time! Or you can swallow that false pride and be *really* smart.

Those who get somewhere in life usually do it by "dealing" – give a little, take a little – not by bulldozing ahead. You can get what you want more often by making the effort to come half- way. If you want to question rules and regulations, do it with "sweet reason" rather than by a fight. Accepting one rule be- cause it makes sense, but giving reasoned arguments against another because it doesn't, is far more effective than trying to throw them all out because "Rules are boring!"

When you have something you want to say, it's often very easy to lay out your points beforehand. But face to face with the person, all those clever words vanish! You may forget someth- ing, or feel so out of your depth that you back down. This can happen with a doctor, a teacher or anyone you have to see form- ally. The best way round this problem is to *write down* the points you want to make. If you have it in writing, you can jog your memory. You can even insist that you stay until all your ques- tions are answered or your statements heard. Try it – it works!

Above all, remember that when an adult gives you a bad time, it's very often not because of something you have done or because you are an unpleasant person. It's more likely to be because he or she is feeling angry at teenagers or even the world in general. The trick, as always, is to:

1) Understand
2) Negotiate – offer to deal.

Teenagers often complain that adults don't respect or under- stand *them*. Perhaps this is because both understanding and re- spect have to be two-way!

15. The National Health And Your Health

'**I** hate doctors. Mine treats me like a child – he usually talks to my Mum and acts as if I'm not even there! If I had something personal wrong with me, I'd never go to him, I suppose I'd just suffer. And my dentist is even worse – he never talks at all! But you've got no choice, have you? And you can't complain about them, 'cos they're doing you a favour' – Terri M.

When you see a doctor, you don't actually give him or her money for the service. But in fact, you *do* pay him or her for seeing you! Each family gives about £18 a week in taxes to the National Health Service. The idea of doing it like this is so that no-one will ever be put off asking for help with an illness because they have no money. Unfortunately, we tend to forget this indirect way of paying, and look on treatment as a charity rather than a service each one of us is entitled to have.

The money you or your parents pay gives you the right to ask for free medical help. It also funds services for your eyes and teeth.

If you are under 16, your doctor is chosen for you by your parents. That doesn't mean, however, that the doctor can tell them everything you've said or that you have to accept treatment if you disagree with what your parents want. For instance, if you ask for birth control your doctor can refuse to give it to you. But unless you give permission, he or she shouldn't tell your parents you have asked for it. If you are pregnant and your parents insist on an abortion "to save their faces" or that you must keep the baby "to teach you a lesson", your doctor can listen to what you want and do what is medically and emotionally right for *you*. If your parents' religion prevents certain treatment but you don't share their beliefs, a doctor can help you in

an emergency, or seek a Court Order to have permission to treat you in spite of what they insist.

At 16 you can choose your own doctor. Your old family doctor might find it difficult to recognize that you are no longer a child.

Most doctors, though, can see a change and, when you get to be 15 or 16, start talking directly to you or even ask your Mum to wait outside while you explain what is bothering you. But some still discuss everything with your parents – and you might prefer the privacy you *are* supposed to have. To find a new one, get the list of doctors in your area from a main Post Office or from The Family Practitioner Committee – a group of people responsible for local G.P.'s (look under "Family" in the 'phone book). Or look under "Physicians" in the Yellow Pages. Or ask your friends! Any doctor must see and treat you if you are ill enough to be in danger, but doesn't have to take you on as a patient for good. If you can't find a surgery to take you, contact the F.P.C. because they must find you one.

You can change your doctor at any time and you don't have to give a reason. If you have moved, even to the next street, you just take your Medical Card to the new doctor and ask to be taken on their list. (If you've lost your card or never seen it, contact the F.P.C. and they will help you get a new one). Usually, if you haven't moved, you must either ask your old doctor to sign the card or you can write to the F.P.C. saying you want to change and giving the name of the doctor you would like to see. It will take 2 weeks from the time they receive the letter – this is to stop people chopping and changing too often. If you do this too many times, you may find doctors refuse to take you on!

A doctor must "render to his patients necessary and appropriate personal medical services". This means they must see you themselves or arrange for a deputy, do their best to diagnose and treat illnesses, visit you if you are too ill to come to them and send you to a specialist if necessary. It *doesn't* mean they are gods and can always cure you! If a doctor has a good reason to think you aren't all that ill, they can refuse to visit and don't have to send you to a hospital. Neither does a doctor have to give you a prescription – only if they think it necessary. You *can* expect to be seen by a doctor if you have an appointment. Or if you have an illness that needs immediate attention. Or you get to the surgery in time for a non-appointment visit. But if your doctor only sees patients by appointment and your problem can wait, they are within their rights to make you an appointment for another time.

Most doctors are caring people who will do their best to listen to you and help you. You may be unlucky enough to get a bad deal, however. Some doctors can be impatient and arrogant. Just because you are young or female, they might decide you're faking it or your symptoms are "all in the mind". A wise doctor will know you need sympathy and advice for problems with emotional as well as physical causes. But some doctors are so blinkered by these beliefs that they will ignore physical symptoms just because of your age or sex.

So, if *you* know there is something bothering you, and your doctor won't take you seriously, *don't* give up. Keep on at him or her, or ask for a "second opinion". Under the NHS rules, if you do this, you must be sent to another doctor for their opinion. Or move to another doctor. If a shop gave you bad service, you'd take your custom elsewhere. Your doctor is paid a fee by the government for every person on his or her list. If you're not happy, vote with your feet and make sure that payment goes to a doctor who does treat you with respect.

The only services a doctor can charge for are things that do not actually affect your health. They can ask for a fee for writing a sickness certificate or for giving you a vaccination for foreign travel if it is not needed and writing out the vaccination certificate. They can also charge for giving you a check-up and writing out the report on it for insurance or a new employer.

All necessary medicines are paid for by the N.H.S. and you usually only have to pay a Prescription Fee – a charge per item to cover some of the costs. In reality, the price of most items is a lot more than you give each time. For instance, a course of antibiotics can really cost £10 and some medicines are as much as £50 a bottle! On the other hand, some things you may be prescribed – such as a cough syrup for a cold – are available "over the counter" at less money, so it is always worth asking the chemist about this. Prescriptions are absolutely free if you are: under 16; retired (60+ for a woman, 65+ for a man); pregnant;

have a child under 1 year old; have a low income or receive Family Income Supplement or Supplementary Benefit, or have a medical condition such as epilepsy or diabetes. Birth control is free to everyone.

Hospital treatment is also free under the N.H.S. and there are three ways of getting it: in an emergency, when you will be rushed to hospital in an ambulance (you don't have much choice about this situation!) Or you can take yourself to an Accident or Casualty Department – most hospitals have one. These deal with emergency cases, where the illness or injury is too severe to be dealt with by a G.P. or when your own doctor is unavailable or you are too far away to get to them. For this reason, Casualty Departments can refuse to see you if your problem has been going on for some time or if it is trivial and they feel you would come to no harm waiting to see your own G.P. But, of course, if it is serious, you will be seen by the proper specialist and given any tests or treatment you need.

Other than in an emergency, the only way you can see a hospital specialist is through your own doctor. Your doctor has to give you, or send to the hospital, a "Referral letter". In this, your doctor says what they think is wrong with you and why they want you seen.

The exceptions are if you visit a Venereal or Sexually Transmitted Disease Clinic – also called a "special" clinic – or a Family Planning or Well Woman Clinic. All these will see you without a referral and keep your visit private if you don't want your doctor to know.

While you are in hospital all treatment and medicines will be free. Normally, they wouldn't ask you whether you agree to the tests they will carry out – it's taken for granted that, since you're there, you give your consent to anything that will help to make you well. They will ask you or your parents to sign a form if you are going to have an operation. But you can question any procedures and make up your mind whether or not to have it – and refuse if you like. Of course, if you do refuse treatment they can ask you to leave! You will usually be asked if you mind having medical students present during any examination and you can refuse this. You can leave a hospital at any time, unless you are there with certain infectious diseases – such as typhoid or smallpox! If you find an open ward hard to take, you can pay for an "Amenity Bed". The treatment you get will be exactly the same, but you will have privacy in a room of your own.

You can ask your own doctor or hospital for any information about your illness, but they don't have to answer you. Your medical records are not yours but the property of the Health Authority, and only if you are suing them – for wrongful treatment, for instance – can you get a court order to see them. Even then, you may only have the right to ask a friendly doctor or lawyer to look at the records. In practice, most doctors have the sense now to realize that patients often get well quicker if they understand what is going on.

If you are unlucky enough to have a handicap or have an accident that will keep you at home for some time, there is help available. You can get a home help to do housework and home nursing if you need it. You can have "Meals-on-Wheels", be given priority in housing and have various adaptations – ramps, grab rails etc. – fitted free. You can have equipment – bedding, clothing, walking sticks or deaf aids as needed – provided. You can have help to buy and adapt a car, or an invalid vehicle and special parking stickers. Holidays and outings can be free or very cheap, and you can be given a free television or radio. None of this could make up for your misfortune, but it could make life more bearable.

Apart from medical or surgical treatment and aids for medical problems, the N.H.S. also provides help with your eyesight. Eye tests are free from opticians and you can have one every six months or as necessary. For your very first visit you need a referral from your G.P. or school health staff, but for further visits you can go direct. If you need glasses, the N.H.S., in addition to paying the optician's fee, will pay for part of the cost of the lens – that's the actual glass part. These are carefully and specially made for you, to fit your eyes. You also have to pay for the frames – the cost depends on the style. If you want more attractive, private frames you can have your N.H.S. lenses fitted in them by the optician or at a shop. All N.H.S. costs are free if you are under 16, still in full-time education or have a low income. You can get contact lenses on the N.H.S. only if there are very good reasons why you can't use glasses.

A recent change now means you *can* get your lenses as well as the frames made up for you by a wide range of shops if you are over 16. All you have to do is take them a recent "prescription": the special description of what your eyes need, as tested by an optician. It may be cheaper to go to a shop. However, opticians spend 2 to 4 years learning their jobs and they are the experts. Your eyes can change quite quickly, so a prescription that fitted last year may now be wrong. There are quite a few eye problems that an optician would spot – and a shop miss or ignore. Save money, by all means, but don't do so at the expense of your sight or health.

Dental services are also provided by the N.H.S. Unlike with doctors, you actually only "sign on" with a dentist for a course of treatment and you can go to a new one without any fuss or bother. Of course, it does make sense and save time if you stick to one. The F.P.C. has no obligation to find you a dentist, as it does to find you a doctor. If you are unlucky and are refused by all the dentists in your area, you are on your own and will have to look further afield. Like doctors, lists of dentists are found at main Post Offices, at the F.P.C. office or in Yellow Pages under "Dental Surgeons". When you go to a dentist, make sure you say you want N.H.S. treatment. The dentist doesn't have to treat you under the N.H.S. and unless you say so, they can "assume" you are going for private treatment! Not many would do this, of course, but you could be unlucky!

Under the N.H.S., a check-up and examination is free, but you have to pay a part of any treatment, up to a set maximum, for ordinary care such as fillings. If you need a crown, bridge or dentures, you will have to pay the full N.H.S. cost for them. But if you are under 16, in full-time education, pregnant or have a child under 1 year old or a low income, all treatment, even dentures, is free. Another way of getting entirely free dental services is to go to a dental hospital. You may be seen by students –

under strict supervision! – or young dentists getting experience, or a lecturer or even a Professor demonstrating. You may have to wait in a queue, though. Emergency dental treatment can be a problem. Most hospitals have a dental department, but dentists are not always available at "unsocial" hours.

You are entitled to a free check-up every six months. If you are under 21, pregnant, or have a child under 1 year old, you can have a check-up every 4 months.

The N.H.S. can also help you with emotional or psychological problems. Some G.P.s are trained to counsel people with problems. Ask yours – you may be pleasantly surprised to find out how helpful your doctor can be. If you need more help, psychiatric treatment can be had, free, from general or specialist hospitals. You can be an outpatient – staying at home and just going in to see the doctors for treatment – or you can become a short- or long-term patient and stay as long as you need. To get this help you must go to your G.P., who will refer you and make an appointment. If you are seriously depressed and fear you may do yourself or someone else harm and you can't get in touch with your doctor, you can go to a Casualty Department. If you choose to ask for help and become a "voluntary" patient, you have the right to leave the hospital at any time. But if someone else has called a doctor and had you admitted against your will because they thought you were about to harm yourself or others, you will only be able to leave when the doctors think you are ready.

If you think you've had a rough deal from anyone working for the N.H.S., you do have the right to complain and ask for an explanation. You can ask your local Community Health Council about this. Their job is to be watchdogs over the N.H.S., and they will tell you how and to whom to complain, help you to understand your rights and advise and support you. You will find your local one in the 'phone book either under "Community" or by name. For instance, "Islington C.H.C." is listed under "I". You can also ask for help from the Patients Association or MIND.

Remember! You or your parents *pay* for the N.H.S., and you

are entitled to what it has to offer. But never abuse the N.H.S. Don't, for instance, collect a medicine you have no intention of taking on the grounds that "It's mine – I've paid for it!" Every year, millions of pounds worth of medicines and medical services are wasted while things we all need are subject to financial cuts. But the N.H.S. *is* yours, so always feel free to ask for advice when you are worried.

16. Do I Need To Diet?

'My body was normal until I was 13, and then I suddenly got fat. Since then, it's been a constant battle to keep slim. Somedays I just wish I could relax and enjoy life like most of my friends seem to do. Then I get on the scales, and all I can think about is losing those extra pounds' – Hazel D.

If you can't climb a flight of stairs without panting and your thighs are so fat they rub together and produce sores, then obviously you are damaging your health by carrying too much weight about. But many women – particularly teenagers – who go on a diet are not, by any medical definition, overweight. Many, however, feel that the shape of their bodies is "wrong". To make such a judgement, of course, you have to compare yourself against a body you consider "right" . . . and how do you choose which ones are right?

In Western society in the 1980s, we all tend to share the same view of what is a beautiful body. The perfect woman is supposed to be slim, have even features and be fairly tall. If you are square and dumpy, have an unusual chin or nose and are short, you are out of step. So, each year, we spend time, effort and money on buying clothes and make-up, trying to change ourselves to fit; to be the same as all those models and pop stars we see in magazines, papers and on the cinema and TV screens. A glance at history books, in art galleries or even at old films, would show you that what *we* think of as beautiful would have looked skinny or ugly to earlier eyes. Some of the Old Masters, for instance, liked their women to be an armful – look at the pictures painted by the artist Rubens to see this. And the women who were idolized in the early days of the cinema seem chubby today.

Today, we set our standards by the women used in advertisements – "models". But the looks needed to show off clothes and other goods to their best advantage are not necessarily attractive features in real life. To make a dress hang well, to show its line and the material, a skinny "clothes horse" is better than a more naturally rounded body. And a photograph always makes people look fatter . . . so models have to be thin.

This can cause quite a problem. Because, just as you are reaching an age when your looks matter to you, two things happen: you start to notice that the world seems to be saying "thin is beautiful", and puberty starts. The first thing that happens during puberty is that your body starts gathering a layer of fat, in preparation for your change from a child into an adult. This layer of fat is an essential part of growing up. Women's bodies, although not meant to be fat, *are* meant to have curves. Men's bodies often put on a similar, if thinner, layer before this firms up and becomes muscle. But the change can be frightening and annoying to you. Not only is your body the "wrong" shape when you compare it to yourself last year, it's the "wrong" shape when you look at the magazines. So, many of you reach for the diet sheet.

Dieting is dangerous if you try it before your body has actually finished settling down from this change from child into adult. If you try to lose weight now, at the time when that layer of fat is needed to nourish your body through the great transformation, you could stop the process and even damage yourself. A woman's body needs a certain proportion of fat before periods will begin. Lose that fat, and periods may be delayed or stop. This is why your parents tell you: "It's only puppy fat – it will go away." They're right! They're not jealous of your youth and looks. They're telling you truthfully to hang in there and wait for nature to take its course. When your body has matured, the extra fat will change into the proper, mature outline for an adult.

Some young people are so confused and frightened by the changes at puberty that they refuse food as a way of getting control over their bodies. They look in a mirror and see a stranger taking over. They see fat where anyone else sees skin and bones.

They can even starve themselves to the point of death. This is now recognized as a type of illness and given a medical name – Anorexia Nervosa. Getting obsessed with dieting too young can lead you into this illness, so beware!

True anorexia happens for many reasons. In some people, it can happen just because dieting gets out of hand. If you starve yourself, you can get to a point where you feel light-headed or "euphoric". You no longer feel hungry. In fact, the sight of food might make you feel sick! With some girls, anorexia is a way of staying like a child, since dramatic weight loss removes those womanly breasts and hips that puberty gives you. In others, it is a way of getting freedom from over-protective parents. Refusing a mother's food is a way of saying: "I can do without you!" It can also be a way of getting control. You might have no say in many parts of your life – your parents can divorce, send you away or even die. But you can seize control over your rebellious body and force it to do without food!

A good guide as to whether you have gone too far is if you have had regular periods and they suddenly stop or come in fits and starts. If this happens after you have been on a diet, think *very* carefully about what you are doing.

But if you do feel overweight and you're beyond the age when puppy fat should have melted away – which is 2 to 4 years after your periods started – then what should you do? Will a diet work?

Going on a diet seems a logical way to lose weight. The principle behind it is this. The body converts foods into energy and any extra is stored as fat. Cut down on food and the body should start running on those fat stores. However, it's not quite as simple as that! You must remember that our bodies still think we are apes living in caves, not knowing where the next meal is coming from! The fat stores are hoarded until the very last moment. If you suddenly reduce your food intake by going on a crash diet, the body takes steps to look after itself. Rather than give up fat, the first thing that is released is water and a form of sugar stored in the muscles. You feel tired, and all your body processes slow down. Your body does this to save energy. You then need less food to stay in the same state. And as soon as you give in to your body, which is crying out for you to replenish those lost stocks of sugar, you will probably gain weight again. This is because you will go back to eating a normal amount while your body is still burning energy at that lower rate. What is worse, some of the weight you lost was muscle and tissue protein, and this could be replaced with fat. So your crash diet lost you a few pounds for a few days, and made you feel weak. But you have ended up at the *same* weight but with *more* fat on you than before.

Losing weight over a long stretch of time avoids most of the harmful effects of a crash diet and usually works. As long as you manage to use up more energy than you take in fuel, you should gradually burn up fat stores. But if the only way you try to slim is by limiting your food, you're always at risk of giving in to that fatal treat! The biggest problem for a dedicated slimmer is battling with those feelings of guilt and unhappiness when you do give in to a craving. Feeling miserable because you want something or guilty because you had it is no way to spend your life!

Most diets offer a miracle cure – a way to slim without effort. Not having to "work hard" seems to be what we all want. Which is a pity, because it can be fun (yes, fun!) to slim, if you put some physical effort into it! Some foods contain more energy or are more easily changed into fat than others. So the way to lose unnecessary weight is simple: cut down on those harmful foods. The ones to avoid are anything with fat or sugar in them. Fat is found in oil, lard, whole milk, butter, margarine, cream and, of course, the fat on meat. So you need to limit anything fried, whole milk and many types of cheese. You should cut out butter, or at least spread it thinly, try to refuse cream cakes and trim the fat off your meat. Go for chicken and white fish, which are lower in fat than red meat. Sugar is mostly found in sweets (obviously!), cakes and biscuits (which are also high in fats) and in soft drinks and alcohol. All the fats and sugars you need for a healthy diet are available in lean meat, skimmed milk, low-fat cheese and fresh fruit and vegetables. Brown, wholemeal bread is very good for you, as long as you don't smother it in butter or margarine (in spite of the ads, still high in fat), or jam! Potatoes are also good, as long as they aren't fried, as is pasta.

But you don't have to cut out all the things you love, as long as you aim for a daily menu that gives you variety and keep to the other part of losing weight – increasing your energy output. The reason that exercise, especially aerobics, became so popular is because some clever souls proved something energetic people had known for some time: that regular exercise gets your "metabolism", that is your body processes, ticking over at a higher rate. Someone who is doing regular exercise is burning up more energy than a lazy person *even when they are sleeping*! You won't see a good sportswoman or man who is fat. Muscled perhaps, but not fat. And a woman's muscles don't bulge, but produce a trim, attractive body. There aren't many fat pop stars either. This isn't because of dieting but because they're always on the go. If you were lucky (yes, lucky!) enough to go to a school where they made you do sports, you probably have less of a weight problem than friends who were allowed to be lazy. And many teenagers find their worst weight problems begin when school sports lessons stop. But getting fit can be such fun! It can give you a good social life, and rather than making you tired, a good work out in a swimming pool, squash court or keep-fit class makes you feel pepped up and full of energy. If you do exercise that gets you puffed for at least 20 minutes, 3 times a week, after a few weeks your body will begin to burn up your food; getting you and keeping you slim and trim. At this stage, you can feed yourself occasional fattening foods without their going straight to your waistline.

The two most important steps to take are to realize that the word "diet" shouldn't just mean a punishing and strict regime that you only keep to for a short time. Your diet is what you eat every day for the rest of your life. If you want to be fit, healthy and full of energy, you would do better to experiment with all the tasty foods that *are* good for you. And secondly, join the thousands of people who have found that exercise isn't a bore!

Make some sort of sport – a keep-fit class, a daily jog or swim, a regular game of squash – a part of your life. Do this, and you can forget about "diets" for ever . . . you won't need them!

17. It All Helps The Party Along: Drugs, Legal And Otherwise

'**W**e were always given warnings at school about drugs and the dreadful things they'd do to you. But they'd never *tell* you, in detail, what they meant. Me Mam and Dad smoked and had the odd drink and I sort of took all that for granted. "Drugs" to me meant something that was really expensive and hard to get, the way everyone talked about them. So when I was given something at a party and it made me feel good, I didn't think there was anything to be worried about. It was for free, a bit of fun to help the party along, just like the booze. I wish I knew than what I know now' – Jerry D.

We all know what a drug addict is like, don't we? He's young, scruffy and dirty. He gets his illegal drugs from pushers, and hangs around unsavoury places like Piccadilly Circus in London or the rough end of your town. He's unemployed, so he's also likely to be a criminal. Right?

Wrong! Because most drug addicts in this country look like you, your parents or your friends. Their drugs are legal and seen as perfectly normal by everyone around them. This may sound incredible, but the fact is that the drugs that cause most problems in our society today are alcohol, tobacco and tranquillizers. A drink, a cigarette and the odd pill from the doctor – we take them for granted. It can be very difficult to understand how *they* could be harmful.

Drinking is a part of nearly everyone's life. If we go to a disco, a friend's house, a party or a pub, it's assumed that you will have a drink. If you ask for a soft drink or refuse outright, you're liable to be teased or even bullied: "Don't be a wimp", "Don't be a baby". If you are under 16, you are not allowed to buy or drink beer or cider in a public place. If you are under 18, the same applies to spirits. Yet most of us start drinking in public at

SPOT THE DRUG ADDICT

ANSWER: Nos 1 2 3 4 5 6

a much earlier age. You *can* legally drink in private – at somebody's home – from the tender age of 5. But how much good it would do you is another matter.

What does drink actually do to you? Alcohol may make you feel lively but, in fact, it is a "depressant". This means it slows down part of your brain. It acts on that bit that normally makes you feel shy and quiet, so most people find it helps them feel happy and relaxed. When you drink, the alcohol goes into your stomach. If you have just eaten, some may be absorbed by the food. But if you are empty, it will pass straight through the stomach into your blood stream. The blood is pumped into your liver, where much of the alcohol is burned off. But the liver can only cope with a small amount; what is left goes to the brain. The more you drink, the more the level of alcohol in your blood rises and the more your brain is affected. Your judgement gradually goes and your reactions slow down. You often don't realize what is happening because being drunk makes you feel confident and stops you from worrying.

Alcohol stays in the blood for a long time. It takes the liver 2 hours to "burn off" one pint of beer. So, if you've had a drink at lunch time, an evening drink will "top up" the first bout. You may find yourself unexpectedly drunk on only a few glasses. Some drinks are stronger than others. A half-pint of beer equals a glass of wine or sherry or a measure of spirits in strength. After only two drinks – that's 1 pint of beer or 2 spirits – your chances of having an accident at work, at home or in a car increase. After 5 drinks, you are 4 times as likely to have an accident, and will be over the legal limit for driving. At 10 drinks, your speech will be slurred, you will be noisy and perhaps quarrelsome and be 25 times as likely to have an accident. At 13 drinks, you will have double vision and be out of control. You'll probably be unable to remember anything about what happened when you wake up next day. 16 drinks will put you in a coma. 25 will kill you.

But this is only a rough guide. Your age, your body weight, how quickly you drink, whether you have eaten and how used you are to alcohol, will all play a part. So will your sex, as women's bodies can handle alcohol less easily. If you have a heavy night and drink more booze than you are used to, you may well get a hangover. Your stomach may be irritated and you may feel sick. Your head may ache and you could still feel dizzy. Hangovers are nothing to laugh about – they are your body's natural complaint against being mistreated. Some people recommend "the hair of the dog". All having another drink will do is "top up" the alcohol still in your blood and make you drunk again. You may then not notice the unpleasant symptoms, but they are there, waiting for you to sober up.

If you made a habit of drunken nights out, in time you would seriously damage your stomach, your liver and your brain. But you could do just as much harm by regularly drinking what might seem a small amount. An adult who drinks 4 pints, or their equivalent, a day will almost certainly have problems with their health, their job and their family. For instance, alcohol plays a part in 60% of cases of child cruelty. The worst thing about alcohol is that you can become addicted to it. This means that your body gets so used to regular amounts that you feel awful if you stop drinking. Regular drinkers find that they have to drink, or they are sick and can get "the shakes". They also become unable to face real life without the pleasant haze of being slightly drunk. As time goes on, they need more and more alcohol to get the same effect. But don't be fooled. A drunk doesn't have to be a staggering, filthy old man on two bottles a day. Some people – especially if you're young – can get addicted on as little as *one* pint of beer a day. And when you are addicted, everything – friends, family, job or studies and your own health – will come second best to the need to drink. Drunks are never as much fun to be with as they think they are. An alcoholic is not only a danger to himself, but a misery to everyone around him.

If all this sounds a bit gloomy, remember that there is nothing wrong with having the odd drink. But if you want to remain in control of yourself and your life, you should follow a few commonsense rules. Never drink alone or on an empty stomach. Decide your limit and refuse to let anyone bully you into having more. Drinking in rounds is a bad idea. It may seem a nice, friendly way to behave, but it makes it impossible to drink at your own pace. Above all, you should never think it makes you odd or immature if you refuse to drink alcohol. A lot of really sophisticated women and macho men now drink mineral water or fruit juice because it's healthier.

Thinking it makes you seem older is also the reason why most people start smoking. Drinking small amounts can even be good for you – but *any* level of smoking is harmful. If you smoke you are twice as likely to get sick and are far less fit than a non-smoker. Tobacco smoke contains substances which reduce the amount of oxygen your blood can carry. It also irritates your air passages and lungs. Some of the chemicals will make your blood less likely to clot and others may narrow the blood passages or arteries. All this will mean that you will become breathless and suffer from coughs and chest infections. You also have a far higher chance of having a heart attack, a stroke or a lung disease when you are older. The longer and more heavily you smoke, the greater your chance of becoming ill or dying early. 1 in 4 smokers dies from an illness caused by their smoking.

The problem is that, once you start smoking, you become addicted to one of the chemicals in the tobacco – nicotine. When you inhale a lungful of tobacco smoke, the nicotine is taken into your blood along with life-giving oxygen. Nicotine affects the heart and the brain, and makes you feel alert if you are tired, or relaxed if you are tense. This may feel nice at the time, but the more you smoke, the worse you feel between cigarettes and the more you need to smoke. It's a vicious circle.

Some girls are afraid to give up because they have heard that you can get fat. This has some truth. Smokers are often thin because the nicotine makes your pulse race and your body may speed up and burn off extra calories. When you give up, the craving can drive you to nibble sweets, and obviously you will put on weight. But other people have found that they feel so well when they kick the habit that they can take up a sport that they couldn't manage before. Stopping smoking makes them fitter and healthier and they stay slim. 8 million people in the UK have given up "the weed" in the last few years, which proves it can be done.

Smoking is hardly "daring" or sophisticated. Smokers are

smelly. Their breath, clothes and hair reek of stale ash. They cough and gasp and have to spend all their money on cigarettes. Non-smokers can taste their food properly, run for a bus without falling over in a wheezing heap and can afford the latest things. Just as with alcohol, the younger and lighter you are, the fewer cigarettes it takes to get you hooked. Nowadays, there are twice as many non-smokers as smokers, so you shouldn't have to feel you are unusual. Smokers are a dying breed – in all senses!

You'd hardly think that a doctor would give you something that might do you harm, but the fact is that many people – especially women – become hooked on drugs from their doctors. Some people find that they feel sad or anxious, or have difficulties relaxing or sleeping. It can be very tempting for a busy doctor to hand over pills which seem to cure these worries. And it can be very easy to get used to sweeping any problems "under the carpet" by taking a calming pill. But these pills can actually make things worse. For a start, many problems will not go away if ignored, but will only get worse. If you are depressed because you can't get on with your family, for instance, it would be far better to get help to sort this out than hiding your feelings. If you get used to taking pills, you lose the knack of solving problems and getting on with people. Mothers alone with young children find that, far from calming them down, the drugs remove their self-control: when they do get annoyed, they can batter their children. Others get so used to being in a haze that if they try to stop the pills, the sudden rush of real, live emotions is frightening. More and more doctors are now trying to limit the pills they prescribe and only give such drugs for a short period, to tide someone over a particularly bad time.

The fact that these three types of drugs are easy to get, and are taken for granted by everyone, often makes it very difficult for you to see the dangers and work out what you really want to do. Advertisements, television shows and maybe your friends make using them seem so attractive and natural. But whatever they tell you, the fact is that the sorts of illnesses and problems they could bring *you* are not pretty and are not fun. It's your body and your life, so make your own mind up and don't let others tell you what you should do.

When you are young and taking your first steps in the adult world, it can be exciting to do things that you know "the grown-ups" wouldn't like. Staying out late, using Dad's stereo, drinking in a pub when you are under age – half of the fun is *because* you know it is forbidden and you want to see what it's like. Taking illegal drugs can be part of this too. If your group of friends experiments with tobacco, alcohol or sex, those are the things you will use to show you are no longer a child. But if someone in your group uses other drugs you may find yourself drawn into something you *won't* be able to handle, whatever comforting lies they tell you.

Some people start using drugs in this way just because it's the "kick" available and it's something new to try. Some try them because they are depressed – family, school or work problems are just too much. They find certain drugs will make them feel happy and forget their problems for a time. The drugs usually offered are pills, LSD, cannabis, heroin, cocaine and solvents.

The pills are often got from doctors. The tablets themselves are not illegal if used as medicine – only if misused in this way. They can be "uppers" or "downers". Uppers make you feel lively and can keep you awake and excited for hours. "Dexies", "blues" or "purple hearts", "black bombers" or "meth" are all types of "speed". You may have seen graffiti which says: "Speed kills!" This doesn't mean fast cars, but these sorts of pills. The problem with speed is that when the drug wears off, you feel not only very tired but also depressed. You might feel tempted to take another, to make you feel better, and end up collapsing. Speed use can also lead to brain damage.

"Downers" make you feel relaxed and will drown out any worries. They can be drugs such as Valium, Mandrax ("mandies") or Nembutal. Valium, which is taken on doctor's prescription by thousands of ordinary mums, is now known to be addictive. You may feel happy while you are taking them. But when you stop, not only do your worries return but your body craves for the drug and makes you feel uneasy and even sick unless you take another. Nembutal is far worse than Valium as it is a barbiturate, a type of drug to which you get addicted very quickly. Also, "barbs" and Mandrax react with alcohol, so if you pop pills and drink at the same time, as many idiots will encourage you to do, you may feel extra good and relaxed – before you collapse from an overdose. Any pop-music historian can reel off lists of names – Jimmy Hendrix, Phil Lynott, Jim Morrison, Janis Joplin, Keith Moon who made this fatal mistake.

One of the greatest dangers of accepting these pills at a party, apart from the real risk of getting addicted, is that since you will have no idea exactly how strong a dose you are being offered, you could overdose. Pills come in all shapes and sizes. They can be white, yellow or blue tablets. They can be green, yellow, orange, or orange and blue capsules. They can be large, medium or small in size. The size is no clue to how powerful the drug is! You can become addicted even if you only use pills at the weekend, and you *can* overdose on one tiny pill. An overdose could put you in a coma – a very deep form of unconsciousness. It could stop your heart or damage your brain. Many deaths in drug users happen because the person passes out, vomits and then chokes to death.

LSD or "acid" was the "Hippy" drug of the 60's, but is again becoming popular. It makes you hallucinate and everything seems more intense and enlarged. An acid user can spend hours staring at a raindrop and can believe he or she has found the secrets of the universe. This would be called a "good trip". But acid can also lead to "bad trips", when a minute seems like hours and the user feels as if the whole world is attacking them. Acid use can tip a seemingly sane person over into psychosis or a form of madness. Since the amount of acid needed is so small, it can be impossible to judge the dose. Acid can come in a capsule or a tiny square of gelatine called a "window". It can also be soaked in a sugar cube, a piece of blotting paper or any other absorbent material. All sorts of other more dangerous chemicals can also be sold as LSD. Trips can last from a few minutes to hours. A nasty side-effect can be "flashing", where the user can suddenly and unexpectedly have all the sensations of a trip, days, weeks or even months after the last dose. This can be far from pleasant or funny even if it was a good trip. It could happen in the middle of crossing a road or in an important exam or job interview.

Cannabis is a drug which many people think is either harmless or far less dangerous than booze or tobacco! It certainly isn't in the same category as the other drugs we are looking at. Cannabis comes from a plant – hemp. The leaves or stems can be smoked on their own and are called marijuana, "grass", "ganja", "weed" or "pot". A cannabis cigarette is called a "joint". A more concentrated form is called resin – usually known as 'hash'. This comes as dark brown or black lumps that look like Oxo cubes. This is crumbled and mixed with tobacco or smoked on its own in special small pipes. Cannabis can make you feel "high" – happy, relaxed and carefree. It is not addictive, although a frequent user may get to the state where he or she cannot face real life without it. Cannabis might eventually harm your heart and lungs. It could certainly harm your life: it is illegal and if you are caught with some you could end up with a police record. One of the dangers is that if you smoke cannabis you may be coming into contact with people using other, more dangerous drugs. They may have their own reasons for wanting you to move on to using these.

The most dangerous drug available is heroin. While 10 years ago heroin was really only a problem for a small number of very troubled and unhappy people, it is now being offered and pushed to thousands of ordinary British teenagers. Heroin is known as "skag", "smack" or "horse". It comes as a white or light brown powder that can be mixed with water and heated to dissolve, then injected with a needle and syringe. The drug can be injected into a vein or just "popped" under the skin. Or the powder itself can be heated and the smoke inhaled. This is called "chasing" or "chasing the dragon". Users may tell you that "skin popping" or "chasing" are safe and you won't get "hooked". You are hooked – or addicted – when your body needs the drug so much that without it you feel sick, have the cramps and feel itchy all the time. It is easy to get hooked because the first "buzz" or "high" feels marvellous and the "down" when the drug wears off is not too bad. But after only a few doses, the buzz gets less and the down gets worse. This will go on until the user is fully addicted and no longer really feels good. The drug is only necessary to keep away the ghastly effects of coming down. What's worse, more and more of the drug will be needed to make you high. A person using one dose at first will soon be needing 5 or 6 or more. This stage is usually reached within *one month* of starting on the drug. 'Skaggies', or heroin users, are your biggest danger because they *need* their drugs so badly that they *have* to get supplies, or money for supplies, daily. They often can't do proper work, so they steal or go into prostitution. Or they sell drugs to other people. They may have an arrangement so that for every four doses they sell, they keep one. This makes them very keen to sell to *you*. Heroin now costs as little as £5 a dose. But you could quickly have a £200 a week habit and have your life shortened and ruined. Heroin addicts don't live very long, especially as the expensive white powder is often mixed by the dealers or the pushers with cheaper chemicals such as chalk and strychnine. They die from the effects of the drug, blood clots in their ruined veins or infections caught from dirty needles.

In fact, you can come off heroin. In spite of what films and newspaper stories may say, the "cold turkey" of stopping the drugs isn't as horrific as you might think. You would feel as if you had a very bad dose of 'flu. You might get diarrhoea, feel sick, be unable to sleep and have a runny nose for a few days. If you could grit your teeth and stick it out, you'd soon be back to normal. The trouble is that, with instant relief only a needle away, many addicts don't have the courage to put up with a few days' unpleasantness.

Cocaine or "coke" also used to be injected but is now usually sniffed or inhaled – known as "snorting". Cocaine comes as a white powder. While heroin is a dull colour like talcum powder, cocaine is shiny or crystalline – like sugar. Today, because of its use by some pop stars, it has become very fashionable – and very expensive. We're not yet sure if you can get physically hooked on coke, but you can certainly get to the stage where you need it to make you feel good. Use it a lot, however, and you will find you have a permanent running nose and eventually the flesh between your nostrils actually gets eaten away – very unpleasant!

You could also get problems with your blood circulation if you use it for any length of time. Cocaine gives you a feeling of energy and makes you able to concentrate, which is why artists, writers and composers are among the people to use it. The danger is that you can depend too much on the false abilities the drug seems to give you and become unable to think on your own. There have been fine artists and performers whose work has gone steadily downhill. Through a haze of drugs, it might have seemed fine to them and anyone else who was "high". But anyone with a sober mind could sadly see it was rubbish.

All the drugs we have mentioned cost money. A modern and cheap method of getting high is solvents. Glue, Tipp-ex, lighter fuel and many other ordinary household products contain chemicals which, when sniffed, can make you feel good. The stuff is poured into a bag which is placed over the nose and mouth and the chemicals breathed in. But these chemicals can give you brain damage or stop your heart, and quite a few glue sniffers have died from these causes. Others have died from being sick and choking on vomit or suffocating in the plastic bags, or having accidents when high and out of control.

Why do people take drugs? Sometimes, they're used as an escape. If life is boring or you think you have no future, you could be tempted to find excitement or escape in the dreams and feelings a drug can give you. Sometimes, they're used as an addition, to heighten experiences such as a good party or concert. Whether you use cigarettes, alcohol, pills, pot or scag, you could be doing the same thing – lightening your day or dulling the pain of daily existence. It may seem a clever, daring thing to do. It isn't. You wouldn't think much of an adult who still needed a dummy to suck, would you? Taking cover behind drugs from the real world and its pains and problem is just as childish.

Drugs may seem fun and exciting. Because you know someone who takes them and seems in control and happy you can be fooled into thinking your parents are just being fussy and boring if they warn you. They are not. "Something to help the party along" will soon become "something to help the weekend along". The nice friends who shared their pills and their "joints" and offered you a "free taste" would soon be selling you drugs your body couldn't do without. You'd swear: "I could stop if I wanted to" and very quickly forget to say anything, because all you'd think about is how to get the next "fix" or dose.

Drugs *aren't* fun. Life can be just as exciting without a haze of chemicals to add a false brightness. However gloomy and hopeless you feel, drugs won't solve problems but only give you more. A life with drugs can only get worse. A life without can always be better.

18. Troubled Minds

'I was in with a crazy bunch at school. Mad Annie, I was called and there was Crazy Kate, Loopy Lizzy, Nutsy Nan and Daft Debbie. Even the teachers called us mad and we had great fun. Then my Mum had a breakdown and it wasn't funny anymore. It seemed that all those words were good for a laugh until they got *real* – and then nobody wanted to know' – Annie L.

1 in 9 of you are likely to suffer from some kind of mental illness during your lifetime. 1 in 3 will know someone – a relative or a friend – who will do so. So it's rather sad, isn't it, that we throw words like "crazy" and "mad" around as jokes, but have some pretty odd ideas about those illnesses and how they affect people. The illness itself may hurt a victim. Our attitudes and lack of understanding can hurt them even more.

So what *is* mental illness? For a start, it's *not* the same as mental handicap. Someone is mentally handicapped when their brain doesn't work as well or grow up as quickly as most people's. This could mean, for instance, that it takes them weeks to learn something you can understand in an hour. Or they might reach the age of 12 and yet still only understand things in the way a young child can. We call this "having a mental age of three or four" or whatever. Most people with a mental handicap are born with it. Serious illnesses such as meningitis or an accident that damages the brain can also cause handicap. But, in most cases, the baby's brain is damaged during pregnancy. Perhaps the mother unfortunately catches German Measles or has a hormone deficiency. In some cases the "genes" are damaged. These are minute blueprints which carry all the information which decides what colour hair and eyes, what sort of body and what sort of intelligence the baby will have. These can have an in-built or "genetic" fault. If this happens, the baby can be men-

tally handicapped in many ways, the most well known being Down's Syndrome or Mongolism. A difficult birth or one where the baby doesn't start breathing in time can also result in damage or handicap.

Not all handicap sufferers have the same level of difficulty. It can range from making someone a bit slow on the uptake right through to preventing them from doing anything for themselves. Mental handicap can't be *cured*. Given loving support and encouragement, many handicapped people can slowly learn everyday practical skills and may be able to live and work like you or I.

On the other hand, mental illness can happen to anyone, and is very rarely due to physical or inborn causes. To understand mental illness, it is worth thinking about the sort of moods you go through all the time. Sometimes you may feel happy enough to burst. Sometimes everything seems so black and hopeless you wish you could die. Most of the time you're somewhere in between. Even the blackest mood passes as you put whatever caused it behind you and remember good times. Mental illness is when these extremes of feeling get out of hand and can no

longer be controlled. It's when not only can you not shrug off
unhappy feelings, but when they come as a reaction to unimportant events. A person who is becoming ill in this way will, for
instance, react to breaking a cup in the same way as you might if
you were told your father had died.

There are two basic types of mental illness, which doctors call
"neuroses" and "psychoses". Most of us know a neurotic illness
by its popular name – a mental or nervous breakdown. This
usually happens when a person has been put under a lot of
stress. Perhaps exams are looming and they're afraid of failing.
Perhaps their job is going badly or they're even out of work. Or
life at home is difficult and parents are getting at them. Or their
wife, husband or children are getting on their nerves and not
understanding their feelings. Unhappiness will then become
out of control and become "depression". If a person is depressed, they are more than just miserable. They feel that everything is useless and that they are worthless. The slightest comment which seems like criticism, or asks them to do something
they feel is too much, will trigger off rage or tears. They may feel
too tired or weak to even get up from bed or a chair. They may
forget to wash or eat and just sit, staring into space and thinking
of nothing. The simplest task – writing a letter, cooking a meal,
going to the shops – seems impossible. They may feel that they
might do it badly and are terrified of making a fool of themselves. So they often do less and less. As they get out of the habit
of these everyday tasks, it *does* get more difficult, which con-
vinces the depressed person that their fears were right! Some
people in this miserable state of mind become extremely frightened of certain things, such as open spaces or spiders or dogs.
Some start repeating actions again and again, like washing their
hands a hundred times a day or cleaning the home from top to
bottom. They can become convinced that if they stop, something dreadful will happen.

Sometimes a nervous breakdown becomes worse, and then
the doctors call it a "psychotic disorder". In this situation, the
sufferer may feel so useless that he can be certain everyone
would be happier if he kills himself. In some cases, his moods get

so out of control that they swing from total misery to almost frightening happiness. When such a person is down, his speech is dull and he moves and thinks slowly. But the following day he could be in an "up" phase, dashing around and chattering so quickly you may not be able to keep up. Sometimes a person with a psychosis becomes convinced that "they" are out to get him. He may think that people on the street are following or talking about him. Or that friends or family are plotting behind his back. He may even think that they are planning to poison him. Sometimes he becomes "schizophrenic" or, as it is often put, has a split personality. This does not mean that he has two different personalities but that his thinking is jumbled up. He may believe that his actions and thoughts are controlled by an outside force and he can often see, hear, taste, smell and touch things that aren't there.

Most mental illnesses can be cured. Since they happen because the sufferers have lost the ability to cope with certain problems, the best way to cure the illness is to tackle the problems! A depressed person may be seen by a family doctor, a hospital doctor or a trained counsellor. He may stay in hospital or just go in for treatment. Mostly he will talk about his feelings and problems and gradually work out why they have come to this state. In some cases, drugs will be used to control the unhappiness until the worst is past. Unfortunately, this takes time and effort on everyone's part and some doctors just don't have such time or the training or understanding to do it. So, they just give the drugs. This might cover up the misery but does not solve the real problems.

Someone who is suffering in these ways can be very frightening and embarrassing. You may find them difficult to be with because they are so sad and will refuse your attempts to cheer them up. Or they may be extra touchy and shout or cry at what seemed to you to be a simple comment or request. They can do odd things like laugh at funerals or cry at parties, and you may want to slide away and ignore them. Mental illness is thought to be rather shameful and something to hide or ignore. If a member of your family went into hospital with a broken leg, you would tell all your friends. If it was with a nervous breakdown, you are more likely to lie about it. And you may have good reason, because most people would share your fear and shame. Someone who has had such a breakdown may find it very difficult to find a job or rent a home – nobody wants to be near them.

It's worth trying to understand and be more sympathetic to people in this situation. If you put pressure on a bone, it will crack. And while it's healing, people will be kind and helpful. Minds crack under pressure too. You can't catch a mental illness any more than you can catch a broken leg. Most mentally ill people are very unlikely to harm *you* – it's themselves they can hurt. So we should try to treat this illness the way we do any other – with sympathy and understanding. After all, it *could* happen to you.

19. When A Fear Gets Out Of Control

'I used to blush whenever a teacher asked me a question. It got so bad that I was spending my whole time dreading being asked anything and I'd bunk off school for days at a time. I know it was silly, but every time I felt my face go hot my heart would pound and I really thought I was going to die' – Elaine R.

All of us have special fears. Spiders, snakes, having to speak in public – all those could make your palms sweat and your pulse race. Being nervous is one thing. Having a "phobia" is quite another. It can be very easy to let ordinary, natural reactions get out of hand and develop into a phobia.

Phobia is the Greek for fear. As long as 3,000 years ago it was recognized that most of us have an instinctive fear of certain things – and sometimes those fears become unreasonable and uncontrollable. All animals – and human beings are animals too – are born with reactions that will make us shy away from any-thing that could cause us harm. Loud noises, flashes of light, sudden scuttling movements, could all be warnings of danger. Our fear helps us to survive these dangers.

When you are frightened, your heart pounds, you may tremble, blush and then go pale, feel sick, sweat and even have an embarrassing and sudden urge to go to the loo. Some people find their muscles tense and they want to run. Some feel horribly weak and just want to collapse in a heap. All of these are the body's instinctive reactions to protect you from peril. When your brain sends a signal saying "DANGER", your body reacts by flooding your system with a hormone called adrenalin. This re-leases an enormous amount of energy and makes you ready for sudden and violent action – Flight or Fight. Emptying your bladder is part of this preparation . . . lightening the load, so to

speak! You blush and then go pale because your body starts
feeding that energy to vital spots using your blood as a carrier.
Energy is needed by your muscles (for strength) and by your
vital organs (to keep them going at double time). When you are
in this state, you can perform physical feats quite impossible to

you at other times. There have been cases reported of men and women lifting weights, jumping gaps and running distances that would have been impossible without the enormous stimulus of fear.

An animal may run from a threat. Or it may crouch down and try to blend in with its surroundings, hoping the menace will pass it by. This is why we sometimes "freeze". A rabbit pursued by a fox, or a baby bird by a cat, knows it cannot outrun its faster opponent, so it relies on camouflage. The instinct to freeze is stronger in some of us than the instinct to run.

But being frightened of things that can harm us is one thing. A phobia is when our fears become out of hand and, rather than keeping us safe, do us harm. Someone who has a real "arachnophobia" or fear of spiders is not just going to be startled and scream when they see a spider skittering across the floor. The true sufferer goes into a panic, with pounding heart, pale skin and shaking hands even at the thought of spiders or a hint that there may be some nearby. The sight of a plastic one, or cobwebs, will produce the same reaction as a real, live scuttling web spinner.

How do phobias happen? In some cases, it can be because of a particular scary incident. You can become deeply frightened, for instance, of dogs, cats or birds, if one hurts or frightens you. A panic-stricken bird flapping about your bedroom, or a bite from a nervous dog, or a friendly cat almost suffocating you in your pram, can all lead to panic at the time and forever after. If you are helped to face the thing that frightened you, you are likely to be able to get your fears under control. Meeting and touching a friendly animal in safety can reassure you. But if nobody realizes what has happened, or everyone gives in to your panic and protects you from any further contact, you have no chance to get over it. You will brood on the event, and it will become more and more terrifying in your memory. It also becomes more and more difficult to even think of the thing that scared you without a panic reaction.

A phobia can also start because something deeply upsetting happens and the object becomes linked in your mind with your unhappiness. For instance, many people find the smell of hospital antiseptics makes them feel sick and frightened – because it brings back memories of the death of someone they loved, or a painful illness. The smell does not actually make them remember why they should feel like this, it just makes them feel miserable and unwell. In most people this is just uncomfortable. In some, it is so bad that they cannot and will not step inside a hospital or doctor's surgery. In other cases, the link is difficult to see. For instance, you may have a horror of fur coats or some other object that could not possibly have done you any harm. But perhaps you have a buried memory of a person or a situation which made you very unhappy. Someone you disliked intensely, who made you feel stupid and clumsy and dislikeable. All those miserable feelings may become linked in your mind with the fur coat that cruel person wore. Quite a few people grow up with dreadful phobias about eating in restaurants – because they had been nagged and made to feel awkward and ugly by parents or teachers at table. These feelings remain and surface whenever they feel unfriendly eyes may be watching them eat.

Lots of people become terrified of blushing. Sudden, unexpected flushes can take you by surprise during your teenage years. A blush can happen because of the way your hormones are still practising their job. A tiny jolt of unease – at being asked a question in class or having to walk across a crowded room – sets off a surge of adrenalin that makes the blood rush to your face. It is also because you feel especially sensitive about your body and your appearance, so you think everyone is staring at you when, in fact, they're not. But if someone *does* tease you about your flushed cheeks, you may tense up so much the next time you think they're looking your way that it happens again. And again. The silly thing is that *you* often notice the blush more than other people. They're usually too busy worrying about their own rosy cheeks to see yours!

Fears and anxieties can be a nuisance. Screaming and flapping your hands around every time you see a spider or mouse can lead to your being teased and will certainly slow up the spring cleaning! But a true phobia can really spoil your life. Phobics are not only frightened when they see the thing that scares them, they become one-track-minded and spend their whole life thinking about it. In some cases they will go to crazy extremes to avoid having to face a dog, a cat or whatever it is. Most of them *know* their fears are overdone, but just cannot help what they are doing. The more everyday and familiar the thing that scares them, the more often their misery shows . . . and the less sympathy they will get. Most of us will not share their feelings and be unable to see "what the fuss is about".

One of the commonest phobias, which usually affects women and often starts in the teens, is agoraphobia. *Agora* is the Greek for "market place" – and this phobia is a terror of going out of the house. Some agoraphobics say they are especially frightened of crowded places. Their first attack might have been in a shop or a busy street. Some say it is of the open sky and describe having a sudden wave of fear on an open hilltop or in a wide field with hedges or fences out of sight. In many cases, agoraphobia starts soon after a dramatic event in the family. Perhaps it was the death of a parent or other relative or someone leaving home, a move to a strange area, or divorce. Doctors say that most agoraphobia is not so much fear of the outside as a fear of leaving the security of your own four walls.

Agoraphobia will start with a panic attack that can seem to be so dramatic and painful that the victim thinks she is dying. Once home and safe, the dreadful feelings go away . . . and a vicious circle will begin. Brooding on the agony, the victim becomes terrified it will happen again. She works herself up into such a state that when she *does* go out the sensations appear on cue. The longer she puts off going out, the more she will build up her fears and the more panic-stricken she is likely to be when she does try it. Most people with phobias know that they are not really likely to die from fright and that they are over-reacting. Knowing this does not always help. What will often happen is that they become so ashamed of their "silliness" that, rather than confess and ask for help, they hide what is happening. Most agoraphobics have a long and convincing list of excuses to explain why they won't come out "this time" or "just now". Parents, friends or even husbands and children may not even realize what is going on but just adapt and rearrange behaviour to fit in with the housebound parent.

Another common phobia is the fear of illness and death. When you are young you do not really understand about death. You find it hard to accept that the world actually existed before you arrived, and really believe you will live forever. During your teenage years, you learn to understand about many things. Hand in hand with an awareness of how babies are made is an understanding that one day you will die. *Many* teenagers have fears about brain tumours and cancer, and become convinced that every headache, pain and ache is a sign of a terminal disease. Such worries are normal at this age, but in some people they get out of hand. Someone with a severe illness phobia may frequently visit a doctor. Each time they are assured that they are healthy and their fears misplaced, they will go home and convince themselves that the doctor missed a vital sign or didn't examine them properly. Some people will go to extreme lengths to keep healthy – avoiding anyone who is sick even if the illness is not catching, and going really overboard about cleanliness.

It can sometimes be quite tempting to pretend to have a phobia. If you make a great fuss and convince people you are scared you may get a lot of attention. But crying "wolf" is never a good idea. People soon realize if you are only having them on, and then they won't respond if you *do* need help. Obsessions about illness are especially dangerous since, if you *do* develop a serious illness, even your doctor may dismiss your real symptoms as having an emotional rather than a physical cause.

If you or a friend has a phobia, how can it be cured? For a start, telling the sufferer to pull their socks up and not be silly is cruel and useless. Taunts and practical jokes may make you feel clever and superior, but will not help the sufferer. Gentle encouragement, however, will make a difference. Facing fears with the support of a friend, letting the terror wash over you and then realizing you are still safe and unharmed, is the best way. An agoraphobic, for instance, should practise stepping outside their front door, clinging tightly to the arm of someone prepared to help. Each day, the distance travelled should get longer, and each day the wave of panic will be less, as the sufferer realizes that fear does not really kill you after all. If your fear is of snakes, spiders or dogs, reading about them and looking at pictures can gradually extend to meeting such creatures while they are safely behind bars, glass or on a leash. Finally, you will be able to touch and handle them without fear.

Fears about blushing are best handled by making a joke about them: "There I go again, isn't it silly!" You'll probably find all your friends will heave a sigh of relief that you are prepared to laugh about it and will also confess how much it worries them. If it worries *all* of you, then you can hardly be silly or unusual to feel this way, can you?

Some doctors may prescribe tranquillizers to help you. This is all very well if the aim is to help you calm down and learn to control your fear as you try to come to terms with it. But if you use the drug to cover up your worries and continue to run away, all that will happen is that you will go on being terrified *and* become dependent on those drugs.

Some people can overcome their fears and life will go on as usual. In some, the hard work will produce an interesting reaction. A dog- or snake-hater will come to love the animal they feared. They may go on to work with them, or own and collect the creatures they dreaded. People afraid of water may practice swimming or sailing so much that they become experts. In other cases, the fear continues but actually gives pleasure instead of pain. People afraid of heights have become climbers or parachutists. They find the rush of adrenalin can actually become addictive. Those who enjoy and are good at dangerous sports will often honestly admit that they are terrified – and that is *why* they do it!

It is quite natural to be afraid of many things. Our ancestors would never have survived if they strolled, whistling, past a sabre-toothed tiger or ignored the patter of tiny tarantula-spider feet. A real phobia is neither silly nor a "put-on". Nor is it your fault. It is a genuine illness that needs as much sympathy and care to make it get better as if you had a broken leg or measles.

If you or someone you know has fears that are unreasonable and prevent them living a normal life, the message is simple: they are *not* unusual or alone and they *can* be helped.

20. A Death In The Family

'I suppose everyone thinks about death at some time or other. You wonder what it will be like – will there be a heaven and hell, or will it just be a misty nothing? Will you know what is happening to the people you leave behind? But I never really thought of it as being *real*. I never thought that someone *I* love would pass on. Horrible things like that only happen to other people. So when I lost my Dad, I just couldn't believe it had really happened. It was a bad joke, a bad dream, it wasn't *real*!' – Hilary M.

Death is one of our society's big "taboos". If you ask questions or want to talk about *this* subject, you're likely to be hushed. You may be told: "You're morbid", which means you have a sick interest in it. Just as with sex, another taboo and equally fascinating subject, we use lots of different words about death to avoid facing it head on. We say that someone has "passed on" or "passed away" or "been lost", rather than that they've died. Few people get to the age of 20 without knowing someone who dies. It might be a grandparent or another relative, or even a parent. A friend may die from an illness, or be killed in an accident. Yet, in spite of this, you are unlikely to be prepared for what will happen.

You might think that your main feeling will be sadness. If so, a death might throw you. Because, as well as sadness, you are more than likely to feel:

Disbelief
  Guilt
    Anger
      Fear and
        Shock.

Death often takes us by surprise. Even if the person has been ill for some time, the way we refuse to think and talk about the

possibility of it means that we can get caught out. Some deaths, of course, are sudden. We often react by refusing to believe they have happened. We may say, or actually fool ourselves into believing, it's all just a bad joke or a mistake: "They've gone away and will come back soon." Parents will often try to protect their children from the sadness of someone dying by telling them this lie. The problem is that you can be hurt even more by thinking that Grandma or your Dad has stopped loving you and never wants to see you again than by the truth.

It sounds silly, but *most* people also feel guilty at a death. They think: "If only I'd been nicer to her, hadn't had that row . . . made him give up smoking . . . take medicine . . . done my homework on time . . . maybe this wouldn't have happened." Having such feelings is normal, but you shouldn't let them take hold. And, just as you should not blame yourself, neither should you blame others for the death. Of course, if the death *was* caused by murder or dangerous driving, that is a different matter. But blaming a doctor for killing or failing to look after a patient properly is usually wrong. We tend to think these days that medicine is little short of magic. We feel that if a person hasn't been *cured*, they must have been *killed*. In fact, it's often those sad guilt-feelings talking. If I can shift the blame onto somebody else, a little voice says in the back of our mind, then *I* don't have to feel so bad. The answer to this is to tell yourself that people die without *anyone* being to blame.

You can also be furious at the person who has died. After all, all these confused and miserable emotions were caused by them, weren't they? How *dare* they go off and desert you, and make you feel so bad! Such feelings aren't wicked. They're normal and natural and shared by nearly everyone who has someone they love die. On the heels of these feelings comes fear. What if other people as close, or closer, to you were also to die? And doesn't this mean that your life, too, can be ended? With many people, the result of all this is "shock". This is when you become numb. You drift around, unable to do or feel anything. It's all so horrible that one part of your mind blocks off the pain, guilt, fear and anger, and it's as if it was all happening to someone else a long way away.

Everyone, whatever their age, will have these reactions to death. You can have them on losing a grandparent, parent, brother or sister, or friend. Your parents will also feel *exactly* the same. One of their greatest problems may be deciding whether to hide or show their feelings to you. Many parents make the mistake of thinking you would be upset by seeing them in tears. They think the effect of seeing the people who should be strong breaking down would be too much on top of the pain of the death. So, they cry in secret and put on a "brave face". The result of this can often be that you get the impression that they didn't care about the dead person! In turn, *you* might decide to keep your feelings private . . . and *they* then think you are hard or unloving. Death *is* upsetting. The pain is made less, not more, by being shared and brought out. Your upbringing might say that tears are soppy and only weak people cry. What rubbish! The bravest, strongest people do not despise tears. If you cry, your misery will be gradually washed away, and heal in time. Bottle it up inside you and, like a wound, it may well fester.

It can take ages to get over someone's death. For weeks, months or even years, you might still expect them to come through a door. You might think you can see them in a familiar place, or even smell their scent or pipe-smoke. You may find yourself laying the table with an extra place, or putting the kettle on and saying: "Ask Grandad if he wants a cup." The anniversary of a death is a particularly painful time, even if you thought you had got over it. Special family occasions – Christmas, birthdays – can also be agonizing. You are not going mad, it's quite a normal reaction. In time, you will feel love and happy memories, instead of pain, when you think of them. How long this will take depends on all sorts of factors. Your relationship with them, your personality and your age will all have an affect. But the more you can talk about your feelings, the sooner you can replace tears with a fond recall.

Other people's grief at death can be embarrassing. If you find the thought of death frightening, you might be tempted to ignore or avoid a friend or relative in this situation. But would you like them to do this to you? It can help you to face your own fears by being sympathetic and helpful. If you put an arm around them, or say a kind word, and they burst into tears, don't be afraid that you have hurt them. Ignore anyone who says you have! On the contrary, you have probably helped them. Go on giving the comfort they need. "Bereaved" people – those who have had someone close to them die – can be very boring. All they seem to want to do is to talk about the dead person and the things they said or did. This sort of "re-living" is a very important part of coming to terms with someone's death, so put up with it! Most people would expect you to feel cut up at the loss of a parent or sister or brother. Funnily enough, when it's a grandparent, a friend, an adult who is important to you or a girl/boyfriend, they may be less sympathetic or just not realize how shocked and sad you feel. Make it clear when somebody's death *has* touched you.

Going to the funeral is also important. Funerals can be very frightening. When you are young, and even into your teenage years, your parents may refuse to take you. This is a mistake because funerals are a very good way of saying your goodbyes. In the company of others who knew the dead person, you can accept that they really are gone, and then all recall the times you shared, which will ensure that their memory never dies. Funerals can make you miserable and give you nightmares. But *not* going to a funeral and saying farewell is often like not crying – it leaves an unhealed wound and you may regret it.

Don't feel embarrassed about your emotions. If thinking about the dead person makes you want to shout, scream or cry, relax and do so. You might find it helpful to talk to someone outside the family, such as a doctor or a priest. They would be used to dealing with people in this situation and no matter how odd or wicked you thought you were being, they would assure you that most people react in this way! If you would like to speak to someone who has been through exactly what you are suffering, you could contact CRUSE – the National Council for the Widowed and their Children. You might be lucky enough to have a Bereavement Counselling Scheme near you. This would be a group run by a specially trained counsellor to help you and your family, in the company perhaps of other sufferers, get over the pain of your loss. Your local Citizens' Advice Bureau could help you find one.

You might find your friends are a tower of strength while you are getting over the death of someone you love. They may be sympathetic, loving and kind and offer you a shoulder to cry on and a listening ear. They may also run a mile. Some people find the thought of death so frightening that they just don't want to know. It's as if they feared death could be "catching". Or that if they had to listen and accept that it's happened to you, it might happen to them. Even adults can act in this way. Some seem to think that you're only in pain if you cry. So they do their damndest to make sure you don't show anything. They'll forbid anyone to "hurt you" by talking about what has happened in front of you. Of course you'll be hurting, even if no tears are flowing; indeed, it will all be made worse by the fact that everyone seems to want to pretend nothing has occurred. The answer to all this is to speak up. *Tell* your friends, teachers or employers that it would really help if everyone could be patient and kind. They will have to put up with your being upset and needing to talk about your grief for a time. If they can't handle it, that's *their* problem and you shouldn't be made to feel in the wrong.

Death is something that happens to everyone. Whatever else you do in life, the twin facts that you *were* born and *will* die are inescapable. And however painful it may be to lose someone you love, you will come to realize that your life goes on. You are not showing a lack of love or respect by laughing and loving once they are gone. After all, if they returned your love, the best tribute they could ask from you would be that you lived happily on in their memory.

21. When A Family Splits Up

'I can't really remember when my Dad left. It seemed as if we just woke up one morning and he wasn't there. I know they weren't really happy – they were always having rows – but it had never occurred to me that they might get divorced. Everyone's parents row sometimes, don't they? It's a fact of life. I hadn't thought it meant anything, so it stuck in my mind that he'd gone off because he'd got fed up with me. I kept asking Mum if I was good, really good, would Dad come back?' – Steph B.

1 in every 3 marriages now ends in divorce. Realizing that your parents' marriage is breaking up can be frightening. Just as when someone is dying, you can find your emotions are a mixture of disbelief, anger, guilt, fear and shock. The most important fact you should hold on to at this point is: IT ISN'T YOUR FAULT!

Nobody divorces their husband or wife because of anything their teenage children have done. As hard as it may be for you to understand, your parents are not just "Mum" and "Dad". They have a private life, too. They have names other than Mum and Dad and a relationship of their own, quite separate from their role of being your parents. Divorce happens because things can go wrong in this part of their lives. Not because of what happens in the part to do with you.

Why do divorces happen? It can be because the marriage was rocky in the first place. Maybe they "had to get married" and have stayed together for years even though they weren't happy. Maybe they expected that marriage would do something, or be something it wasn't. Maybe, over the years, they have changed and no longer suit each other. Marriages are very, very rarely broken by other people. If there is another woman or man in the picture, the affair is usually the *result* of the relationship breaking down, rather than the cause.

Above all, a divorce shouldn't mean you lose a parent. You can stop being a husband or wife, you can never stop being a Mum or Dad. But one of your parents could try to make this happen. Since both of them may be feeling angry and hurt, they might be tempted to use you to make them feel better. They could want you to stop seeing the parent who is leaving, to punish them. Or they could try to turn you against them, to make themselves feel "in the right". They are both natural, human feelings. And the other person may well have behaved badly. But that is none of *your* business. Their argument is between them, and should have nothing to do with you. This also means that you should not be tempted to interfere or make judgements. Even if you know your parents well, you *can't* share or understand the private, adult relationship they have. But you shouldn't have to accept a total break-up between you and them. You might find it helpful to say: "I know Mum/Dad hurt you dreadfully. But I don't want to take sides for *or* against you. I love you both. Please don't punish me by stopping me seeing him/her."

Of course, you too may be feeling betrayed and hurt. You may feel that the missing parent has left *you*, rather than their husband or wife. You may be convinced that their leaving was your fault. And your reaction to such beliefs could be to feel angry. You may hit out at both your Mum and Dad and find yourself picking quarrels with them both. Some people decide to take sides and refuse to see the parent who has gone. Or they enjoy the weekends or days out with the deserter, nagging endlessly at the parent left behind. A father or mother who only sees you on special occasions can seem much more fun than the one who has to cope with looking after you every day!

Having a part-time or weekend parent can be painful. You'd be less than human if you didn't find it makes you touchy and miserable. The sad thing is that sometimes the parent who has to bear the brunt of your confusion decides that seeing the missing parent is the cause of it all. They then think stopping visits would make everyone happier. In fact, although this might drive your feelings under cover, it will actually make things worse in the long run. So, unless you really have decided that *you* want nothing to do with them, it's worthwhile making your choices heard, and insisting on keeping in contact.

Being part of a "one-parent family" is not unusual. Since 1 in 8 families only have one parent, you're unlikely to be unique in your school or group of friends. It can be hard work. Your poor Mum or Dad will either be running a home *and* earning the money to keep you all, or they'll be trying to make ends meet on a limited amount from the Government or your other parent. Either way, they'll be struggling to be both a father *and* a mother to you. You may have to take on responsibilities for yourself quite early. You'll have to lend a hand in doing housework, shopping and cooking and in making decisions about all sorts of things.

One of the most difficult situations you may have to face after a divorce or the death of a parent is that a new partner may come along. A new husband or wife for them means a new "step-father" or "stepmother" for you. Step parents have the most dreadful image. Fairy stories always show them as wicked and jealous. "Wicked" is rarely the case, but jealous might be true. Faced with a step-Mum or Dad, what do you think you'd feel – and how would you show it? You'd almost certainly feel angry and hurt. This person is taking over from your real mother or father. You would feel jealous on your parent's behalf, at the newcomer taking their place. You'd feel furious at the other parent for letting it happen. You also might blame the new-comer for the marriage breaking up. If you had a secret fear that it was your fault this happened, you'd be even keener on shifting the blame onto someone else! You could also feel jealous on your own behalf. With only one parent, you may well have built up quite a nice, close and cosy relationship. The greater respon-sibilities you've had to take will have made you feel like a par-tner rather than a child. Then along comes this stranger, want-ing to shove you down again into being just a kid with no say in what goes on! So, you would be prickly and difficult. You'd do your best to drive home the fact that he or she is just an outsider trying to take over your real Mum's or Dad's place: "Mum always used real potatoes, not Smash" or "Dad always let us watch horror films" or "When are you going home?" If you found a sneaking liking for the new person, you'd feel guilty at this final betrayal, and probably redouble your efforts to be nasty.

Whether you realize it or not, what may stick in your throat most about your stepparent will be the sexual side of their relationship with your real Mum or Dad. When you grow up with parents, their sex life has probably quietened down by the time you are old enough to be aware of it. That doesn't mean parents *don't* have sex – they do! – but it becomes a part of family routine that you don't notice. And, of course, if they were unhappy in the months or years before their divorce, they may have drifted apart. But, with a new relationship, they'll be going through the honeymoon period. You can hardly avoid realizing that they are enjoying themselves in this way. Most teenagers find the thought of the oldies and the wrinklies having sex disgusting enough, without it being their own Mum or Dad! It's not at all unusual for young people to get their own back by having their own boy- or girlfriends. Some even have sex – (or *pretend* to be having it) – far earlier than they would otherwise have done. Partly this is to make a point and hurt their parents, and partly it's to make the boy or girlfriend give them the love and attention they think they're no longer getting from the parent.

Can you be surprised if stepparents find it hard to handle all this? He or she would feel nervous, even before meeting you. If they loved your Mum or Dad, they'd want to please them by loving and getting on with you. The harder you make it, the more they will try – and the more hurt and angry they will get. The sad part is, whatever you do, you *won't* bring the old days back. But you may make sure that everyone – both of your parents, you new stepparent and you – have a thoroughly miserable time. You may think they deserve it – how dare they split up and try to force a new parent on you without asking your permission! Because you are hurt, it might make you feel better to be joined in your misery. But wouldn't it be better to try to make things work? You can do this by:

1) Reminding your Mum or Dad that you too share this home. This doesn't mean you have a share in their private lives, but it does mean you should be allowed to have your say on the new arrangements.

2) Being honest about *your* feelings – and listening to theirs. "Look, I feel really rotten about all this. I miss my Dad and can't help feeling angry when I see you sitting in his armchair." You may get a clip round the ear for cheek. You may instead get: "I can understand how you feel. I love your Mum and I know I can't take the place of your father, but I'd like to be a friend. For a start, shall we move the furniture around and I'll use this sofa?"

3) If you can, insist on keeping in touch with the parent who has gone. Explain that this is not an attack on the one who is left and the new partner. Your parents' relationship with each other may be finished. Yours, with your Mum or Dad, isn't. But also make a new friendship with your stepparent. You *can* get on with them, without it being a betrayal.

All your difficulties could be multiplied if the new stepparent has children of their own. Not only will this new adult be pushing you out of the spotlight of your parent's attention, they'll also be bringing in their own brats to be your rivals! Most families have their own routines. You might always eat the evening meal from a tray in front of the telly, while your new brothers or sisters are used to sitting around a table. You might have been brought up to expect that everyone does their share in the house, while your new family thinks girls do housework and boys get looked after! Celebrations, like Christmas or birthdays, can become battlegrounds if each group has different traditions about presents, meals and games.

If your parents haven't realized that all these things will lead to arguments, it might be up to you to ask for a family discussion to thrash them all out. It might seem a bit odd to have a full-blown argument about everyday chores, but it *is* important.

The way you live day-to-day is something that grows and gets taken for granted in ordinary family life. You will all be making a new beginning in an *extraordinary* family, and at first nothing should be accepted without being looked at. Routines become unexpectedly important to you because they seem to prove that everything is safe and unchanged. You can end up having a screaming row over how to lay the table or when to open presents on Christmas Day. For the sake of all your feelings, you will need to make compromises, to give and take a little. Changing bedrooms around so you all start out afresh; setting up a chores rota so you all do a fair share of work; choosing the best from each family's traditions, or using traditions from each family turn and turn about – all this will help smooth the path until two separate families become one.

We don't always get on with the families we've grown up with since birth. Even your natural parents, brothers and sisters can get on your nerves and behave very differently and have different tastes to yours. If you can only give it a chance and both understand and put aside your natural anger, distrust and jealousy, you are likely to find that life in a step-family is no worse than life in an ordinary one.

22. A Little Learning

'**S**chool is so *boring*. Who wants to know about sugar production and when the Spanish armada set sail? None of that has anything to do with my life' – Lesley H.

You can have one of three attitudes to school. You might think it a total bore; time spent in school is wasted and keeps you away from the things you really want to do. Or you might just take it for granted; it's not so bad, and since you have no choice, why make a fuss? Or you might be lucky enough to go to a school or have the frame of mind that makes learning new things exciting and fun.

By law, your parents must make sure that you are getting suitable, full-time education between the ages of 5 and 16. They can do this at home if they choose. But if they keep you away from school, they must prove that you *are* being properly educated elsewhere. You, in turn, are entitled to full-time education until the age of 19. You could finish school when you reach 16. If your birthday is between 1 September and 31 January, you can leave at the end of the following Spring term. If it is between 1 February and 31 August, you can leave on the Friday before the Spring Bank Holiday (the last Monday in May). But what happens if you and your parents have different views about when you finish school? If you disagree, this should be something you sort out in discussion, but you do have a lot on your side.

What if you want to stay and your parents insist you leave and get a job? Your parents have care and control of you until you are 18. But you are *entitled* to education until you are 19. With the support and persuasion of your teachers, you should be able to win your parents over. Legally, they can't throw you out or refuse to support you until you are 18. Of course, in very rare cases, really angry parents could make life at home impossible. If this happened to you, you could leave home. The Local Authority and your school would help you to find somewhere to live. This may be at a hostel or with foster parents. A friend's parents may even be willing to help. The cost of food, clothing and rent would be covered by Supplementary Benefit. This can be paid to school students who are "estranged" from their parents, which means that you have disagreed so much that you must move away.

What if your parents want you to stay at school and you wish to leave? Again, since your parents control you, their word goes. However, no school wants to keep someone who is horribly unhappy. If you are unwilling, or unable, to join in classes, you won't be helping yourself or other students. While you are under 16, a school cannot expel you – all they can do is suspend you or send you to another school. After 16, however, they can expel you – and will if you kick up too much fuss. More often, they'd ask to see your parents for a chat about what you really wanted to do.

If you dislike school and want to leave, have a long think before you do so. Is it because you are doing badly? Is it because you dislike a certain teacher? Are most of your friends leaving? Are your parents hard up? It might be better to try and change these factors than to turn your back on school. Or it might be better to leave the school setting for a college, rather than dump education all together. Try and tell your parents how you are feeling, and why. You *can* always have a second chance at education – but it might cost you far more effort than sticking it out the first time around.

What happens at home can affect your school life, too. If your parents are going through a bad time and quarrelling or even splitting up, you can hardly be blamed for not keeping your mind on schoolwork. You might not want to get a label of "deprived child". You may not want to share private sadness with teachers. But a kind or sympathetic master or mistress could make life more bearable if you explained what was going on. Other people's problems sometimes affect you, too. People who are having a hard time at home or school sometimes get their revenge by throwing their weight around. School bullying is frightening and miserable. Bullies are rarely just wicked people. Most of the time, they act that way because *they* are pushed around at home. Or they are made to feel so bad that they take it out on people weaker than themselves. School heads can be helpful. But some are so upset by the idea and think it reflects badly on the way they run their school that they refuse to believe that bullying goes on. Whatever the reason for your being bullied, IT IS NEVER YOUR FAULT. Don't believe a bully who says it is because:

    you wear glasses
    are a "weed"
    talk posh
    have "soft" parents
    are a different race

or a host of other excuses. These may be the reasons why you were picked out from the crowd as a victim. But the real reason is that the bully feels so angry at himself and the world that someone – *anyone* – has to pay. Giving in just makes them do it again, so you have to fight back. You could ask your parents to speak to his or her parents. This may work – they may not realize what is happening and be horrified. Equally, it may be their fault in the first place and they may even agree with the bully's excuse! You could get a big brother, cousin or friend to give the bully a taste of their own medicine. The problem here is that *your* brother may end up fighting an even bigger brother. And what happens when his back is turned? Probably the best action is to organize group resistance. Get together *everyone* who has had trouble from the bully or bullies. There is safety in numbers – bullies *always* rely on being bigger or more numerous than their victims. Corner them, and calmly tell them that if it doesn't stop, the next time you'll all seek revenge. I've never known this fail!

What *is* education? The word covers more than just school learning. In fact, we all spend most of our lives learning something. The aim when you are young is to teach you the bits and pieces that will help you cope with adult life. Different cultures

and civilizations have different needs. Our ancestors needed to learn how to hunt and grow crops. A present-day person living in Outer Mongolia or remote areas in Africa might do better learning these skills than how to do calculus. The problem with modern Western society is that it is *so* complicated that trying to give you a thorough picture becomes impossible. Also, changes happen so fast that teachers and text books can't keep up. There are students graduating today in computer sciences who find, when they start a job, that their knowledge is already out of date!

So, schools try to give you an overall "grounding", rather than the details. The most important lesson you are supposed to learn is not the facts themselves. Old history and remote agriculture may seem irrelevant to you. What your teachers want you to learn is that the world did not start on your birthday and doesn't end at your back gate. They also want you to pick up the knack of gathering facts together and making sense of them. Knowing a list of dates is less important than learning how and where you can find out things you need to know.

Teachers can be a help or a hindrance. Some teachers have a gift. They can make even a subject such as Maths seem exciting and fun. Others can turn you off sex education! Teachers, believe it or not, are human beings just like you. Some go into teaching because they couldn't think of anything else to do with their training. Others really want to help you make sense of this complex world. They have off days when the cat's been sick or the car wouldn't start or they have a splitting headache. So, if you don't like a teacher at first, give them a chance. You hate it when people take only one look at you and ever after say: "Tracy's lazy", "Stuart's stupid" or "Mary doesn't try." Teachers feel just as hurt when *you* turn off after only one lesson with "Sir's bossy" or "Miss is boring." If it doesn't get better, it could be worth a try to ask a teacher to meet you all outside classes and listen to any reasonable criticism you have. Teachers can make mistakes and take a dislike to a particular person, just like anyone else. If you feel you are being picked on or marked unfairly, you can do something about it. Keep a record for a few weeks. Talk to your parents and explain quietly and calmly what is happening. You might ask your parents to take the next step, or you might prefer to do it yourself. Ask to see the teacher and put your case. Most adults approached in such a way may be taken aback, but still listen. They may go off in a huff – but think about what you've said later. If you really feel you've got nowhere, ask to see the Head and put your case to him or her. If several of you share the problem, go in a group, but elect one of you as the main speaker – otherwise it might end up in a shouting match!

Try to keep your eye open for "expectations". This is when people label you or your whole class. For instance, a parent may say: "Our type never gets exams" or "Our family always go to University." Teachers may say: "B stream are always bad at Maths" or "Of course, History is her best subject." Expectations have a way of becoming strait-jackets. Even if you would like to go on, or leave at 16 and go into nursing; even if you enjoy Maths or actually hate History, you can get trapped. Everybody sees what they expect to see and refuses to face the truth. The cure is to *speak out*: "Dad, I would like to go to college, and my teacher thinks I can do it" or "Mum, nursing is what I want to do – University is not for me."

Parents can also be helpful or not with schoolwork. Some parents decide what they'd like you to do, rather than listening to what *you'd* like to do. A father who works with his hands might insist that his child should "do better" and go for an office job. Or he might feel that "What's good enough for me is good enough for you." A parent with a professional qualification might think it shameful for a child to want to learn a craft or not go to university.

So, some parents push. They hover over you doing homework and always ask about your marks. They may even greet a triumph, such as getting 95% in a test or coming 2nd in class, with "Why wasn't it 100%?" or "It will be 1st next, or I'll want to know why." Such parents are usually quick to complain when you do badly, but slow to show pride when you do well. The result is usually the opposite of what they plan. Instead of being fired up to work harder, you back off. Nothing you do will ever please them, so why try? It's less painful to be told off for not trying than to do your best and be told it's not good enough. Again, the way out of this is to *speak up*. Say to your parents – and your teachers too, if they're also playing this game – "I'd try harder if you'd said nice things when I did well, instead of nasty things when I do badly." If the response is: "I would, if you did good work", say: "But I did. You don't have to be perfect to be good. If you want me to be perfect, you've first got to help me feel I can at least do well."

Some other parents try to slow you down. Either they leave you alone and don't encourage you to work at school or on homework, or they even interrupt and get you to work around the house instead. Others will help you bunk off – always happy to give you sick notes or excuses. This can seem a nice, easy way out of hard work. It's not so much fun if you actually *want* to pass an exam or get to college. You might find you need to talk to your parents about what you would like to achieve in life. It might be possible to get a friendly teacher to help you. Some parents are afraid that they will be left behind. They fear that a child who goes on to higher education will despise them because they haven't got "qualifications".

Qualifications are what education is really all about. The problem is that, too often, we concentrate on only one type. A qualification means proof that you can do something. When we talk about these, most of us mean exam passes. These are proof that we know a certain amount of Maths, Science or English. They also prove that you have the ability to learn facts and use them properly – whatever the subject. But, sometimes, other qualifications are even more important. For instance, you may be hopeless at Maths and English, but be able to get on with any animal. A zoo or stables might be far more impressed by a letter from a vet describing this ability than 2 "O" levels! If your school is set on "academic" or book subjects and can't or won't encourage other types of skills, then do so yourself. Book learning is not the only kind that deserves respect. Most modern schools, however, recognize this. They will help you, whatever you are good at.

Choosing which subjects or options you are going to take for CSE or "O" levels is probably one of the most difficult decisions you'll have to make at this age. It could decide what you do later in life. It may also split you up from friends. They probably seem more important *now* than anything in the distant future. You may also back off a particular subject you're good at, because you dislike the teacher. Acting on your likes and dislikes is an excellent way of deciding what to do on a Saturday night. It's not such a good way of working out the rest of your life! So, when it comes to these choices, discuss them with your teachers. If your school doesn't have a proper Careers Master or Mistress, go and see the Careers Officer provided by your local authority. It's their job to listen to you and work out, from all the things you're good at and enjoy, what sort of job would best suit you. With this in mind, you can then choose the combination of exam subjects that would best help you get what you want. There is an amazing range of exams you can now do – far more than the standard English, Maths, French and sciences. You could do Politics, Computer Sciences, Woodwork or many more. If your school cannot offer a teacher in these courses, you could be allowed to go to a local college for the necessary lessons. If you insist, the local authority must help you do this. Most important, *don't* allow anyone to put you off just because you're interested in something that is traditionally not for your sex. Girls make just as good carpenters and engineers as boys; boys are just as good nurses and cooks as girls. It is now *illegal* for anyone to stop you because "Girls/boys don't do that." Your parents will also be helpful. But beware of those "expectations" from them. Your parents may be keen to push you into something they'd have liked to do. Or they may not be up-to-date on your fields of interest. They could still be convinced that you want to be a nurse or policeman, as you'd decided at the age of 12!

Homework may seem a particular strain. The point of asking you to do work outside the class is not to give the teachers an easy time off. Nor is it to spoil your fun either! When you leave school, whatever you do in life, there will be times when you have to organize yourself. Either you'll have to work without someone watching over you, or you'll have to decide yourself when and what to do. Homework gives you practice at this. It helps you to teach yourself how to find out things on your own, without a teacher to give you a quick and easy answer. The *content* of the homework is less important than the fact that you do it yourself. This doesn't mean that you can't ask for help. Learning to ask parents and librarians for advice is also part of these skills. But it does mean that *you* should make the effort.

If you *do* leave school without any qualifications, can you have a second chance? The quick answer is YES. Your only problem would be in choosing from all the options. If you have just left school at 16 and can't find a job, you could get a place on a Youth Training Scheme or YTS. Your fees would be paid and you would be given a weekly wage and help with fares and clothing. Part of the 2 year's course would be in a classroom. Part would be actually working in your chosen job. You can learn any skill, from catering to computers; decorating to bricklaying; typing to social work. At the end of the course, you would get a certificate showing what you have done. Some people criticize this scheme, saying it just gives employers cheap labour – the Government pays your wage, not the firm that employs you. This might be so in some cases, but *you* can't lose out. How many times do you see a job advert which says "experience necessary"? Usually, you can't get the job without experience, which you can't get unless you have the job! After YTS, you *can* say you have experience. And you learn *how* to apply for jobs and how to get on with people as well.

If you leave school early and decide at 19 or more that you want a second chance at training, you can apply for the Training Opportunities Scheme or TOPS. On these courses, like YTS, you have your fees paid and a wage and allowances given to you. If you have a family or dependents to keep, you will get extra money. You can have a skill "topped up". In other words, if you already know a bit, you will go on a refresher course. Or you can start from scratch. Office skills, plumbing, TV maintenance or catering – the range is enormous. TOPS courses are all aimed at getting you a job in your area. If you choose a speciality not in demand, you may have to travel or move to find a course, or change your mind. Neither YTS and TOPS can promise a job after – but they will do their best to help and advise you.

What if you decide that university or college is what you want, but you left school with few or no exam passes? Again, there are an enormous number of ways of getting what you want. As a "mature student" – this usually means over 21 – you will find many universities and polytechnics are less interested in exam results. Instead, they want to know what you have done since leaving school. If you can show that you really mean to study and have made an effort to learn, they can take you without "O" or "A" levels. Mature students can get grants which cover themselves, and their families if they are married.

Another way to catch up on a degree is to take one with the Open University. Some employers are more impressed with an Open University degree than with an Oxford or Cambridge one! This is because "OU" courses are usually done part-time at home. It certainly takes hard work and determination. Students get books and papers through the post, and many lectures are given on radio and television. It usually takes at least 3 or 4 years to complete a degree course, but you can spin it out over as many years as you like, to fit in with other work or bringing up a family. OU courses need *no* entry qualifications.

Colleges of Further Education can accept students for technical or craft subjects – hairdressing or jewellery making, for instance – without formal exams. These courses can lead to City and Guilds qualifications, which are respected everywhere.

Whatever your course, you can usually get a grant to cover fees and living expenses. So lack of money should *never* be a reason for losing out on education.

You will be at secondary school for 5 to 8 years. You will probably be in the big, wide world for another 50 to 80! Since the first short period at school might have quite an effect on how you pass the rest of your life, it does seem to make sense to get what you can out of it, rather than just "get out of it"!

23. The World Owes You A Living?

'**W**hen I left college, I really thought the world owed me a living. I wanted a flat, a car and a stereo. I wanted to spend my time and money on enjoying myself, and I thought I was worth at least £10,000 a year. It was quite a shock to find that nobody else shared this opinion – David S.

Whether you leave school at 16, or university at 22, your aim will be the same – to get a job. All of this chapter applies to girls as well as boys. If you are a girl, you may still believe, or have been brought to expect, that being a wife and mother will be your "job" in life. If so, you'll have to find a rich man to "employ" you! In fact, the majority of women work outside the home. The average mum only takes a *few years* off work, until the kids are at school. If you have two children with an age gap of 3 years, this makes 8 years off. This means, unless you are very unusual, you will work for at least 30 to 40 years of your life! The chapter also applies to college or university leavers as much as school leavers. Looking for a job with one CSE and looking for employment with an Honours Degree only differ in the kind of work you may be offered. The actual techniques of looking for and getting that job are identical!

In our society, we put people in pigeon holes by the work they do. Bottom of the heap are those without a job. It's stupid and unfair, but it's a fact of life. You might be tempted into thinking that qualifications are unimportant and leave school for a well-paid job as soon as possible. Or you may grab out of panic: "If I don't take a job *now*, there won't be any going when I do leave college." Watch out for this catch. At first, jobs which demand no special skills can pay more than skilled work. The point is that, as you get older and go up the scale, skilled work pays more and more. Unskilled work remains the same. So an 18-year-old can earn say £150 a week working with his hands while a friend is paid only £90 for being a bank clerk. However, in 10 years time, the first person is still on the same wage, while the second can be earning three times as much.

You may have heard a lot about unemployment in the last few years. That it's all the fault of this government, or the last. That it's a Tory plot to do the workers down, or a Communist scheme to destroy democracy. It's more likely to be that, today, many of the jobs your parents did are disappearing. A few machines and computers can do the work that used to employ hundreds of people. For this reason, there are fewer jobs for those people with no skill or training. However, there are many *new* jobs created by these machines. The catch is that they have to be done by people with training and skills. You are less likely to get a job if:

1) You have no qualifications at all
2) You aren't willing to be trained
3) You set your mind on one job and refuse to consider anything else
4) You won't move to a new town that offers job prospects.

You are more likely to get a job if:

1) You stay at school and get exams
2) You get some form of higher education or training – a degree, a YTS course, a City and Guilds certificate or an apprenticeship
3) You have some work experience from a Saturday or holiday job or from doing voluntary work
4) You are prepared to try anything – even a job with less importance than the one you'd like
5) You are willing to move away to a new area.

Look at it this way. There *are* jobs available. More people are *in* work than *out* of it. The odds are on your side . . . but you have to swing them your way. For a start, you have to decide what it is you'd like to do. Some people make their decision at 12 and never go back on it. If you are one of these, you may have planned your whole secondary-school education round becoming a doctor, nurse, farmer, mechanic or chef. Some of you only know that you do or don't want to stay on for college, but have no firm plans. But, as the end of your formal education comes nearer – whether at 16 or 22 – you *must* begin to make plans for your future. You don't have to do this on your own. You can enlist the help of a Careers Teacher or Officer. The teacher works in the school. Some teach other subjects and do "careers" as an extra job. For others, it is their full-time responsibility. A Careers Officer works for the Government, and Careers Offices are usually part of the local Council. The advantage of using a Careers Teacher is that they might know you, your talents and strengths. They may be able to suggest jobs you hadn't thought of, by recognizing your skills. They may see you around the school building many times, and be able to think about your needs. The disadvantage may be that, if they are not doing it as a full-time job, they can't know of all the opportunities open to you. Even a full-time, hard working Careers Teacher can get caught if you have a bad name in the school. If *all* the teachers think you are lazy or a quitter, the Careers Teacher might also not realize it's because you've never been trusted or given a chance.

A Careers Officer, on the other hand, starts from the beginning with you. He or she can make a fresh judgement, untouched by past history. An Officer is also more likely to be in touch with the very latest job opportunities and training schemes. However, they won't be able to give you as much time as an "in house" adviser. Also, the Officer's not knowing your abilities can be a drawback if you find it difficult to clearly describe everything you can do.

Whether you go to an Officer or a teacher – or both – the procedure should be the same. Rather than just offering you leaflets, a careers adviser will try to help you work out what you would *like* to do and what you would be *good* at. You will be asked to think about:

The things you do well
The interests and responsibilities you have
The sort of person you are
What you would like from life.

You might be surprised at what a good careers adviser would think important. Being a dab-hand at building model aeroplanes or making cakes are both skills. Knowing that you belong to a karate or swimming club, or that you have total responsibility for feeding the family pet or preparing Saturday tea, can all build up a picture of you. Knowing whether you are the person all your friends come to with problems, whether you do homework without prompting, or whether you are impatient, adds to this picture.

One of the most important types of question you would be asked is which of these you would put top of your list in an ideal job:

Lots of money – or "financial reward"
Being admired for having that particular job – or "status"
Enjoying or getting a kick out of the job – or "job satisfaction"
Knowing that you can stay in the job and won't be sacked – or "job security"

Most jobs and careers score on only one or a few of these points. Hardly any combine four! A nurse, for instance, doesn't make much money. But people do admire nurses. Even more important, a nurse can come home at the end of a day feeling proud of doing something worthwhile. Businessmen might make money, get a kick out of succeeding and be envied and admired. But a business can go bust and that enjoyment be spoilt by stress. Each person has different priorities – so see which are yours. Remember, your working life takes up 40 hours a week, 48 weeks a year, of most of the rest of your life! You may think that you could stand a hateful job as long as it paid well or people looked up to you. But could you?

Once you and your careers adviser know the things you could and would do, he or she may come up with a list of suggested jobs or employers to approach. What next? The first contact you

ALWAYS ADOPT THE CORRECT ATTITUDE WHEN APPLYING FOR A JOB

have with an employer is vital. *You* judge people on the impression they first make on you, don't you? So does a boss. In most
cases, your first contact will be through a letter. You may be

answering an advertisement or you may be writing "on spec" to a firm you'd like to work for. The basic rules are the same:

1) Write your letter out in "rough" first.

2) Follow all the rules of proper letter writing. That is, put your own address at the top right-hand corner, with the date underneath. Put their address lower down on the left. Start with a "Dear Sir" or "Dear Madam", or a name if you have it. Always finish with "Yours faithfully" if you don't have a name, and "Yours sincerely" if you do.

3) In just a few words, explain *where* you found out about them, *what* sort of job you'd like, *why* you want to work for them and *how* you would suit the position.

4) Say when you can come for an interview.

5) Write it out neatly and use the best paper and envelope you can afford.

You may have heard people complaining of sending off hundreds of letters and never having an answer. It's true that adults can be rude and thoughtless. It's true that firms can have so many requests, they don't answer each one. But, if this happens to you more than a few times, it might be worthwhile wondering honestly whether you could be at fault. Scruffy paper and bad handwriting will probably mean your letter is rejected before it is even read. If the letter is too short and sounds like a "formula" – that is, the same letter you have sent to other firms – then it might also be discarded. A prospective boss wants to have a fair and honest picture of the sort of person you are, and the things you can do. He or she also wants to think that you, in turn, have some idea of the work they do. A letter that shows neither of these may well be ignored.

If your letter does "pass", then you may be asked to fill in an "application form". This will ask about your background so far. As well as your full name and address, the form will ask you to list:

Your schools and colleges

Exams passed – with grades
Your work or training experience
Your hobbies or activities
Any achievements.

Be honest about all these – it won't pay to lie! Most of all, remember that exams can take second place to other achievements and qualifications. If you've done volunteer work or a Saturday job, say so. Collecting money for charity in sponsored swims or runs also counts. Winning cups or medals at BMX riding is also something to be proud of. So is helping your parents at their jobs, if they run a shop, a market garden or some other business. Your hobbies also say a lot about you. So, again be truthful about how you spend your time off.

If you are given an interview without needing to fill in such a form, do it for yourself anyway. The chances are that all these questions will come up in the interview. You will find it much easier if you have got your thoughts in order and on paper. This description of what you have done so far is often called a curriculum vitae or "C.V." This means the "path or course of your life". Before the interview, do your homework. The first step to getting a job is showing you have an interest in the organization and the things they do. This means going to your local library and finding out as much as possible. A large organization may publish an Annual Report. Ask to be sent a copy when you fix the interview date. If possible, find some people who work there already and ask them about their jobs and the working conditions. Practise answering the sorts of questions you might get at the interview. The careers adviser, your parents or friends could help with this.

For the interview, look as neat and tidy as possible. You might have thought that leaving school was the time you could get away from "uniforms". It's not as simple as that! The interview is a formal, business meeting, and you will need to dress the right way. After all, you are hoping to impress them that you can fit in and do the job properly. The clothes you'd choose for going to a disco are different to the ones you'd use to slop around at home. In the same way, you need to choose appropriate clothes for the interview.

Be on time for the interview and be polite and friendly to whoever meets you. Many bosses ask their receptionists what *they* thought of applicants – so keep this in mind! Be prepared to shake an offered hand, and remember the interviewer's name. At the interview, answer every question as fully and honestly as possible. Listen carefully, be friendly and smile occasionally. If you are nervous, SAY SO! You won't be "marked down" for such a natural feeling, and you may get points for having the sense and courage to admit it.

At the end of the interview, you may well be asked if you have any questions. Try to work some out beforehand. This shows you have given the job some thought. For example, what about job training? What prospects are there for promotion? What pay and holidays do you get? What sort of people would you work with? What conditions would you work in? If you think you may forget under stress, write them down. If you feel *all* of these questions have been answered already, say: "I had a long list, but you've covered them all, thank you very much." As you leave, offer your hand to be shaken, and thank the interviewer by name.

Your first job might be quite a shock. You have to fit in with new people and new surroundings. You also have to go "back to the beginning". At school, by your last year, you would have been top of the heap. Even at college, you are at least started in company with other new people. But here you may be the only new face, and that can be scary! Go gently at first. You might have a reputation among your friends as a joker, a lover boy or the best thing since sliced bread. But try and push that at new people and you may find yourself disliked. Be friendly to everyone and you will gradually find your own group. A good way to get to know people is to ask advice. This *doesn't* mean getting others to do your job. It does mean saying: "I'm new round here and I'm not sure how you do this usually. Should I . . . ?" or "The boss gave me so many new instructions, I'm a bit muddled. Should I . . . ?" You pay the person a compliment and avoid making mistakes. You also have a good excuse to chat with the person at coffee break, or have them approach you.

If you can't find a job, don't despair. Don't give up and waste your time. Set aside a part of each day to search for jobs and apply for them. It's not enough to wander down to the Job Centre for a glance at the cards. Lots of firms advertise on their own and the Job Centre may have only a small proportion of the jobs available. Look in your local newspaper. Write to large firms in your area "on spec", asking if they have openings. Remember, always include a copy of your "C.V." with any letters you send.

Spend the rest of your day *doing* something. Learn a new skill, volunteer for charity work. Scout around your neighbourhood and see what chances there are of casual work – baby sitting, gardening and window cleaning can all bring you a few bob. They can sometimes also build up into a full-time career. If you have "signed on" and been receiving Supplementary Benefit, you may be able to ask for an Enterprise Allowance to help you do this. This is a scheme to help unemployed people start small businesses of their own.

You might also like to consider travelling further afield for job opportunities. This doesn't mean just getting on a train and expecting the streets of London to be lined with eager employers! You could think about gaining experience by doing Voluntary Service Overseas. Your local firms may not need your skills, but a Third World village may be desperately in need of your teaching abilities, gardening talents or just a strong back! You could find that a few months as an *au pair*, fruit picker or helper in a Summer camp could give you confidence, and a good reference, for finding a job back home.

If you don't go straight from school or college into a job, you should "sign on". This means that you go to a Job Centre and register for work. They will help you fill in 2 forms – one for work (called a UB461) and one for benefit (called a B1). Unemployment benefit or "dole" money is only available to people who have worked for a certain amount of time in the previous year and paid National Insurance contributions. You will more likely be wanting Supplementary Benefit, which is available for anyone who hasn't worked and has no money to live on. You may need to prove how much money you have in a bank or Post Office account and how much you have to pay out on rent and living expenses. Take along any papers you have to prove these things. Both these forms are long and complicated, so don't be put off. Ask for help over questions. If the office can't give it, take the form to the nearest Citizens Advice Bureau – they will help you. If everything is OK, you would get a cheque through the post in about a fortnight. You may have to attend an interview. If the staff feel you are not trying hard enough to find a job, they may give you a hard time. But, if you know you are really trying, you can face them with a clear conscience. Stand up for a fair deal and don't let them put you down. If you *are* doing your best – and only you can know this – then being without a job IS NOT YOUR FAULT!

24. Money, Money, Money . . .

'**M**oney used to be a sore point with me and my parents. All my friends were getting an allowance when I was still on "pocket money". I had to ask each time I wanted *anything*. Then my Dad said it was about time I learned to manage on my own. He was really helpful about it. I made a few mistakes at first – like spending my entire month's money on a concert and having to darn my tights! But I learned' – Tracey U.

Money can be a sore point with most of us! In fact, you may well find that there are more arguments in your family over money than any other subject – including politics, religion and sex! When you are young, "pocket money" is usually all you need

and are likely to get. So, you may be given a small sum to spend on sweets, toys or comics, but everything else will be bought for you *if* your parents agree you can have it! As you get older, there are likely to be more items that you want. Partly this is because you will see friends or advertisements displaying things which tempt you. Partly it is because you *will* have wider interests as you grow up, and want to explore them. Records, books, special clothes or items for a hobby will catch your eye. Partly, however, it will be because the time has come for you to make your own choices and not to have them made by your parents.

At this point, arguments may become bitter. Your parents may feel put upon. It seems to them that all they hear from you is "Gimme, Gimme! I want, I want!" You are also likely to feel resentful. What you ask seems so reasonable – why are they being so mean? Whether they can admit it or not, your parents will be feeling hurt. What is at stake is not a new LP or jacket, but freedom from their control. If you can recognize this and take it into account, a request for more money can be made with success.

What do you need money for? You can split up all your "expenditure" – that is, money spent on you – into the following categories:

1) Entertainment. This covers films, videos, records, tapes, books and magazines, discos and some sports.

2) Eating. This covers sweets, snacks and meals outside the home, and sometimes school meals.

3) Non-essential clothes. This covers latest fashions or clothes for some sports, but not school uniform or everyday clothing.

4) Hobbies and interests. This covers equipment for your interests – model building, BMX, horse riding and some sports.

5) School equipment. This covers pens, rubbers, exercise books and some text books.

6) Christmas and birthday presents for your family and friends.

7) Girls will also want to buy tights and make-up and need to get sanitary protection.

8) Essentials. This covers clothing, both for school and outside, meals when you are away from home and fares for school journeys.

You can divide your expenditure onto 3 basic levels. The top level is the important items, such as overcoats or shoes. These cost a lot of money and you need them. It's fairly reasonable for your parents to want a say in how such objects are bought, until you are quite old. The bottom, third, level covers unimportant and cheap items such as snacks, sweets and comics. The middle level is the one that causes most heartache. These are the medium-priced things that you may or may not need, and *you* want to be able to control. "Pocket money" just covers the third level. An "allowance", however, can cover most of the middle level.

Most parents recognize that you *should* learn to handle your own money. The world is full of unhappy people who make a hash of it. They get into debt and can really ruin their lives. If you are going to make mistakes, it's better to do so as early as possible and learn from them.

You could present this argument to your parents. You could point out that it would make life far easier for them if you were not always asking for things. And it would give you essential practice at coping on your own.

How should you work out a fair allowance? It's no good looking at your friends. Their parents may have more money to spend. Or they may live in a different way and spend their money on different things. The best way is for you and your parents to write down *everything* that is bought for you, or by you, over a period – say 2 months. At the end, divide everything into the categories – entertainment, eating, etc. Then, decide between you which responsibilities will be yours. You might take everything except number 8 – the "Essentials". You might decide on 1 to 4 and 6. Girls may want to buy their own make-up but still put tights and sanitary protection on the weekly family shopping list. Whatever you decide, work out how much your parents have allowed to be spent on these items during the period. Make sure that the time you looked at this is "representative" or a fair judgement of the whole year. For instance, if you looked at December and January and all your family have Winter birthdays, you would come out way ahead of the game! If you listed over a hot Summer, however, you'd miss out on the money normally spent on school books and tights. When you have agreed a fair figure for 2 months, divide it by 8 or 2. This would be the sum you are given each week or month.

You and your parents should each promise certain things. *You* should promise:

1) Not to ask for more money if you spend yours all at once.
2) To keep a written note of how you spend your allowance.
3) To discuss it again every 3 months.

They should promise:

1) Not to interfere in how you spend your allowance.
2) To give you a fair chance before discussing the situation.

After 3 months, you can all "review" what has happened. This means sitting down and looking calmly at what you have bought and how you have managed. You may feel that everything has gone well. You may decide that something was left out of the original adding up and you need a rise. Your parents may feel that you have spent money on things *they* would not have bought. But, if you have kept control, they should be pleased. Any mistakes can be discussed. *Everyone* makes a bad purchase at some time. The trick is to make as few of them as possible, and this may take years to learn. The earlier you start, the better chance you have.

If your parents can't afford as much of an allowance as you'd like, you have 2 choices:

1) Suffer!
2) Get out and earn some money!

Some parents might agree to extra payments for jobs done round the house. They may already give pocket money on the

understanding that some chores are done – feeding pets, mow-
ing the lawn or washing cars. Certain chores are part of life.
You're not a guest in your parents' home, but a member of the
family. Tidying your room, making your bed and helping to
wash up or prepare meals are just a few of the things *everyone* –
boys, girls and fathers – should do as well as the live-in house-
keeper you call Mum! But you could reasonably ask to be paid
for washing windows, polishing floors or digging the garden. In
other words, anything *extra* to everyday living can be the subject
of a deal.

Your parents may still feel justified in putting their foot down
about how you spend *their* money. They can't really complain if
you earn it by "the sweat of your brow". By law, such money
belongs to you and you can spend it as you choose.

You cannot take a part-time job until you are 13 years old.
Between 13 and the time you leave school, you can only work at
certain times. These are different in each area. Your school or
library should be able to tell you the local "bye-laws" about
school-age youngsters and work. On the whole, the rule is that
you can't do more than 2 hours on a school day, and shouldn't
be working before 7 a.m. or after 7 p.m. You can usually work all
day on a Saturday, but not at all on a Sunday. Some work is out
of bounds altogether. You can't work in a bar or pub. You can't
do anything dangerous, or be asked to lift heavy objects. Nor
can you sell door-to-door. Most areas forbid you to work in a:

Betting shop
Billiard saloon
Slaughterhouse
Restaurant
Kitchen or cake shop.

In actual fact, many employers ignore these rules. Paper rounds
often begin before 7 a.m., and strong lads are often put to filling
supermarket shelves. Cafés and local bakeries often rely on
schoolboys or girls. Casual work, such as baby sitting or car
cleaning, is obviously done "out of hours" and for longer than

the time allowed. The rules are only likely to be applied to you if your school or parents are worried. If they feel that your schoolwork is suffering because of a job, you might be stopped.

Your parents might want to reduce your allowance, or stop it all together, if you are working. You may think this is fair if your family is hard up. If you think it unfair, collect your arguments and discuss it with them.

The point of learning how to handle money is that you don't spend it all at once. You learn to "budget", to spin your money out over a period of time and always have enough for the things you need. You can put your cash:

Under your mattress
In a piggy bank
Or in a
    Bank
    Building society or
    Post Office account.

All of these have advantages and disadvantages. Mattresses and piggy banks mean your money is always to hand. This could be useful – or a drawback if you need a little help to stop yourself spending! Your money could also be "borrowed" by family or friends, lost in the Spring cleaning or eaten by the dog. Opening an account may mean you have to organize yourself better. But isn't this the point of learning to handle money?

There are two types of account: "deposit" or savings accounts and "current" accounts. You can open a "deposit" account at any age. They are offered by banks, building societies and the Post Office. When you put or "deposit" your money in such an account, you would be given a small book. This shows all the money you pay in or take out. With some accounts, you have to give "notice", or tell them in advance, if you want to take money out. With others, you can do so when you like. All deposit accounts "pay interest". This means that, since the organization uses your money while it is with them to finance their business deals, they pay you a small fee. This "interest" is usually between 6p and 12p for each pound you leave with them for a year.

Most of them work this amount out each month, so you do get some even if you take your money away sooner. Deposit accounts are useful if you want to save up for something – a stereo or holiday, for instance. If you think you might need to use your money quite a bit, you might find a "current" account is better.

With a current account, you get a cheque book. Instead of getting a book showing all your deposits and withdrawals, you keep a record of these yourself, in the cheque book. You are also sent a "statement" each month. This is a clear list of everything you have done with your account in the month. The big advantage of current accounts is that not only can you take money out at your bank, you can write cheques to pay for things in shops and elsewhere. So you don't have to carry money around. The big drawback to you would probably be this: most shops will not take a cheque instead of money unless you also have a "cheque card". And, in most cases, a bank won't give you one until you are 18. The card is a piece of plastic that shows your signature. The shop can then compare your signature and see that the cheque book is yours and not stolen. It is also the bank's promise to "honour" your cheque – to pay the shop the amount of money shown on the cheque. Because, by law, you can't be made to pay your debts until you are 18, most of the banks will not give you a card until this age. Nor will they give you an "overdraft". An overdraft is when you take out more money than you actually have in your account – it's a sort of loan.

However, a few banks can be flexible. If you have had an account with them for years, if you have shown yourself to be honest and sensible or if they know your parents, a bank *might* trust you early, if you had a good reason for wanting a cheque card. They may, instead, give you a "cash card". This allows you to draw money out of a bank machine at any hour of the day or night. The machine is connected to a computer. It knows exactly how much you have in your account and what you are allowed to draw out, so this is safer for the bank than a cheque card.

The Post Office have their own type of credit account, called the Girobank. You must be 15 or over to use it. Some building societies now also offer a chequing account. Some banks will charge you for using a credit account unless you have a certain amount of money banked. Some ask you to keep £50 or £100 with them. Others just want you to stay "in credit" and not be overdrawn. If you went under their limit, they would charge you a small fee every time you used a cheque. These small sums can add up to quite a large amount if you are not careful.

Banks are now very keen to attract young people, especially college students. They offer book tokens and other gifts if you join them. But the one offering the best gifts may not be the best deal. To decide, the most sensible course of action is to ask. Make an appointment with several bank managers, at branches most convenient to you. Do the same with some building societies. When you meet them, explain your situation and needs. See what they can offer *you*.

Bank managers have a terrible "image". Everyone thinks of them as having two horns and a forked tail! To hear people talk, you would think their whole purpose in life was to be mean. Nothing could be further from the truth. Bank managers can be both sympathetic and understanding. It is actually their business to lend out money. But to make sure it won't be lost or wasted, they must make sure that you can handle it. A bank manager likes nothing more than a sensible person who is prepared to *explain* what he or she is doing with their money, and *asks* for advice. Get to know your bank manager and his staff, and you can be sure that any problem with money will be sorted out.

Once you are a known customer, the Bank feels a certain "obligation" to you. This means if you want to borrow money for a particular purpose – buying a car or making a down payment on a flat – they believe they *should* help you. That is, as long as you have proved you will be sensible and pay them back. A bank can also give you a "reference", a letter saying that "So-and-so has been a customer and has always handled their money matters properly." This can help you with some jobs or getting goods on credit.

The same applies with a building society. At some time in the future, you may want to buy a home. For this, you would need a "Mortgage". A mortgage is a special type of loan. It can be a very large amount, paid back over a long time – as much as 30 years. You pay a heavy fee or "interest" on a mortgage over this time. You can end up paying the society more than twice the amount they have lent you, but how else are you to afford the cost of a home of your own? In fact, the monthly cost is often less than rent would be, and you *do* have something to show at the end! Building societies and some banks will give mortgages to individuals and couples who are earning enough money to afford the payments. However, there can be a waiting list . . . unless you are already a customer of theirs!

Banks and building societies may seem stuffy or frightening places. You may think you really don't need an account now. But the sooner you open one, and the longer you have it, the better off you will be in the future. As far as the bank or society is concerned, you are an unknown quantity. Even a scruffy punk can grow up to be a millionaire! So, believe me, they will take you seriously and be happy to have your custom.

25. The Customer Is Always Right?

'**If you're a teenager, you're always getting ripped off by shops. If you take something back they just refuse to give you your money back and there's nobody to complain to. And even if there was, who'd take your word against an adult?**' – Alexia C.

Most of us at some time in our lives have had an unpleasant experience with a shop or restaurant. Perhaps a heel has come off a new pair of shoes and the shop has refused to give you your money back. Or the dry cleaners lose your favourite jacket and say it can't be helped. Or the bill for your coffee and hamburger is much more than you thought it would be. It is easy to lose your temper, and lose the argument, if you don't know your rights. Because, you *do* have rights. There are plenty of laws to protect the "consumer" – that is *any* person, whatever their age, who buys a service or goods. If you have some idea of how they work, you can make sure *you* don't get ripped off.

By law, anything a shopkeeper sells you must be "fit for their usual use" and "of proper quality". This means, for instance, that shoes or a dress must be able to take normal wear and tear and not fall to pieces within a few days. Of course, if you were sold "evening shoes" and wore them to climb Snowdon, the shopkeeper could claim you were not playing fair. If he sold you a suede "fashion jacket" and you wore it in the rain, you couldn't complain if it leaked. But ordinary coats and shoes should be able to cope with average use. You must complain as soon as things go wrong. If you keep the object for some time, because you feel embarrassed at going back, or are too lazy or hope the damage isn't too great, the shopkeeper can say you have legally "accepted" it as it was. All he needs offer is to do a repair himself or to pay to have it fixed. If you get your skates on

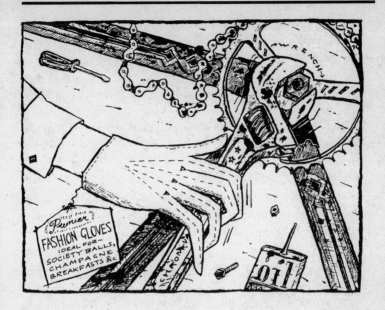

and go back *as soon as you realize there is a fault*, he has to give you your money back or replace the item. You *don't* have to accept a "credit note" (a receipt which means you have to buy another item from him).

If you have gone immediately, and the shopkeeper still gives you trouble, you should send him a letter, stating clearly what happened, and *keep a copy*. If the shop is a member of a trade association, send another copy to the association or the head office. If this fails, go along to the Citizens' Advice Bureau, and they'll help you to take your case to the Small Claims Court. In fact, you'll find that very few shops will let it go this far!

However, if all that happened was that you changed your mind about what you bought, that's another situation. If there is nothing actually wrong, the shop doesn't have to take the item back. Large stores, such as Marks and Spencer, have made it a policy to take things back, because they reckon it pays them in "customers' goodwill". In other words, everybody trusts and likes Marks and a lot of people probably buy more, knowing that they could take it back if they change their minds, than they would have done otherwise. But small shops are often scared you wouldn't buy from them again anyway, so why should they lose this sale? Some will offer a credit note so you can get something else, but they keep the money. In this situation, they are doing you a favour and you *can't* demand the money.

Laws also protect you if you buy on mail order. If the goods arrive and they are not what you expected, you can return them and ask for your money back. You can also demand action if the goods take a long time to arrive. Most mail order firms do say you should expect a reasonable delay – usually 28 days – from when they get your order. If it's much longer than this, you do have the right to complain. You have entered a "contract" with them – in other words, you have promised to buy something, if they promise to deliver it. So you can offer to change your mind, but you must give them notice. What you should do is write to them saying that you want your goods by such and such a date as "time is now of the essence". This means, getting it on time is now the only important thing. If it doesn't come in time, you will reckon that they have broken the contract. If it comes late, you can return it and they must give you your money, or you can refuse to pay an invoice for the goods.

Some firms try to use the post to sell you things. A parcel will arrive and you find it contains a book or a piece of clothing you'd love to have. Then, a few days later, the bill comes! This is called "inertia selling" and it often succeeds because people are too lazy to send the things back, even if they would not have gone out and bought them. You don't have to pay or even send the goods back. But you must do one of two things. Either you should send the firm a letter saying you did not ask for the item and that they must collect it. If they haven't done so in 30 days, it's yours. Or you could just put it away safely and wait. If they don't come within six months, you can have it. But you must be careful not to damage the goods before then, because if they *do* come and it looks as if you have been making use of their property, they *can* then demand that you pay up!

It's not only objects that you can buy, but "services" such as having your clothes dry-cleaned or your stereo repaired. This, too, the law protects. If you and your friends have a snack or a meal out, and the bill comes to more than you expected, it may not be your fault.

Every café and restaurant *has* to display a "tariff". This should hang in the window or doorway and must be visible from the outside. It should say exactly what you can buy inside, and how much it will cost. They either show their prices "inclusive of VAT", which means this tax has already been added into the prices for hamburgers, cokes, etc. Or they must say clearly: "All prices exclusive of VAT at 15%", or whatever the rate is at the time. They must also say if they add a service charge: "Service at 10%", for instance. You only have to pay for what is stated clearly. If they don't list the fact that these charges were going to be added, you can refuse to pay them if they appear on the bill unexpectedly. Mind you, if you didn't bother to look and missed the small print, it's your expensive mistake – or the washing up to do!

If you take an object – a radio or stereo – in for repairs, how much you pay could depend on what you agree to at the time. You might come away thinking it would only cost £10 – and go back to a £50 bill! If you don't watch out, the law may *not* be able to help you. If the repairman says: "It may cost £10" and you say: "I don't mind as long as it's fixed", then he only gave you an estimate and you gave him permission to do anything he thought fit. But if he said: "It will cost you £10" and you said: "That's OK", he gave you a "quote", or a clear price, which you agreed. Having said this, he can't then charge you for work you didn't agree to, or up the bill. Most of the time, of course, we can't clearly remember what was or wasn't said in this kind of situation. So it's always worthwhile insisting on either a quote, which is a fixed price, or a clear, written estimate. This should state approximately how much work has to be done and about how much it will cost. Then he can't try to charge you far more than this. If he does find the job is more complicated and costs more, he has to explain to you and get your say-so before going ahead.

Dry cleaning is another service that causes problems. By law, the cleaner has to "promise" certain things when he takes your clothes, even if this promise is not actually said out loud. One of these things is that he will clean your clothes to the best of his ability. If you think that a stain has not been cleaned properly, you can ask him to try again. You can also insist that crumpled clothes be ironed or a crease put in the right place. The worst thing that can happen is for something to go missing. Another one of those "promises" is that he will take reasonable care of anything left with him, and not allow them to be stolen or lost. Any notice a cleaner puts up saying otherwise doesn't have any effect on his responsibilities under law – especially if the notice would only have been seen by you as you left the shop *after* you had handed over your clothes. So, in this case, the cleaner must pay you the price of the lost clothing. If it is old, he can offer to pay only second-hand rates. But *you* can claim for its being of especial value to you, as long as you are reasonable. If you get any argument, most cleaners belong to an association and you can complain to them.

A tricky situation is if you buy something from a friend or someone you know – and another friend recognizes it as their stolen property! The law protects both you and the original owner in this position. The point is that the article does *not* belong to you now, because nobody can sell an object that does not belong to them. Even if the person who sold it to you was innocent and didn't know it was stolen, the object wasn't theirs to sell. You have to give it back to the owner, but you must also be given your money back by your contact. He or she, in turn, can demand their money from whoever sold it to them, until you get back to the thief. But neither you nor your friend have broken the law, because you had no reason to think you might be "handling stolen goods". Mind, if you buy a solid gold bracelet from a stranger in a pub for a fiver, the Police would have a good case in saying you must have realized it was stolen. So, in this situation, you wouldn't only lose the bracelet to the real owner, you could also end up in court yourself.

Most shopkeepers are decent people who wouldn't think of

trying to cheat you. But there are a few who are not above trying to grab that extra pound or two by giving bad service or selling shoddy goods. You *don't* have to put up with it, because there are laws to protect you, and experts to advise you. Stand up for your rights if you think you've had a raw deal, and don't be afraid to ask for advice from your local Citizens Advice Bureau or Law Centre. After all, it's what they are there for!

26. Far Away Places

'**M**y first holiday with a friend was gross. We were cycling through France and had a row on the second day. We wanted to split up but were too afraid to be on our own. We came home early and didn't speak again for months! It taught me a lot though, and the next time I went away with a friend it was great' – Anthony R.

Even if you enjoy holidays with your parents, sometime during your teenage years you are likely to want to go it alone. School trips might have given you a taste for a break with your friends. Or maybe it's just that you no longer share your parents' idea of a good holiday. Whatever your reason, taking a holiday with a friend or group of friends is very different from spending a Saturday evening with them. It can be 10 times better – or 10 times more awful! You really do need to plan in advance if you are all to enjoy yourselves.

For a start, you need to decide what sort of holiday you would really enjoy. Some peoples' idea of heaven is lying on a beach all day and dancing all night. Others prefer a bit of action thrown in – water skiing or scuba diving. Others like an action-packed holiday like learning to climb, ski or ride. Some people want to travel around by car or bike, while some want to find their resort and stay there! Think carefully about this. You might find that getting a sun-tan is all you really want. But if such holidays with your parents have left you feeling bored, you might find something to get you going would really be more "you".

You could even find a working holiday is fun. Fruit picking in France, being a Summer camp counsellor or helper in America, driving a tractor on a kibbutz or communal farm in Israel, can all be fun. You're unlikely to make much money, but you could have fares paid or food and accommodation arranged. The main advantage is that you get fit, travel and have a pretty hectic social life with people your own age. If you choose to do conservation work in the British countryside or help at an archaeological dig, you'd also have the satisfaction of doing a worthwhile job and learning something.

Holiday firms now offer a startling variety of things you can do both in this country and abroad. You can go to a resort with a few friends and trust to meeting other people on the beach, ski slope or disco. Or you can go on a special group holiday for young people. There are quite a few specialist groups offering "theme" holidays. You can learn or perfect a sport such as tennis, or a skill such as computer operation. Or you can really go for action and learn to canoe, fly or parachute! Some organizations welcome 10 to 18 year olds, but do make a point of separating the older teenagers from the kids and certainly don't treat you like children. Quite a few firms now specialize in offering what amounts to a week-long party for the 18 to 30 year olds. You can go to any of these on your own – you'd be bound to make friends in a few hours! Or, of course, you could just take off with your gear on your back or on a bike and camp or Youth Hostel your way around with a chosen friend. If you decide to go abroad, don't forget to check that you have your own passport. You can get the form from your local Post Office. If you are under 16, your parents will fill it in on your behalf. If you are 16 or 17, at least one parent must add their signature. Apply in plenty of time for the form to be dealt with. The Passport Office gets very busy before the holiday season and delays of 6 weeks or more are quite common.

When you have some idea of what you'd like to do, the next step is to pick a friend or friends. This can be more difficult than you think! Your best friend may be great to share a laugh in class, at work or at a party, but less good when you spend a whole week with them. Try this test. Ask yourself – *honestly*! – which of your friends you would like to have with you:

at a party
on a camping holiday
shipwrecked on a desert island

when you are ill
on a beach holiday
at the cinema
when you feel miserable
when you have a secret you want to share.

You'll probably find that you would choose different friends for most of these. And you may also be surprised at the people you suddenly realize you'd prefer for some occasions. Once you have decided what sort of holiday you want, choose your ideal companion from the result of this kind of test.

When you agreed to go on holiday together, you and your friends should make three promises to each other:

1) Each of you will take it in turns to choose what to do each day. This will stop any arguments about: "But we did what you wanted to do yesterday!" or "But I thought that was what *you* wanted!"

2) If you row, you will have a cooling-off period and then make up. Quarrels are bound to happen when people live side by side. Agree on a code word or joke to put it behind you with no bad feelings.

3) You will respect each others' privacy and separate needs.

There's no point in sticking together like leeches when one of you longs for a swim and the other wants a quiet moment to write postcards. Agree to meet in the bar in an hour and relax! Once you've made the arrangements, stick by them. If another friend suddenly offers a "better deal", don't be tempted. *You'd* hate to be let down at the last moment, wouldn't you? And someone who asks you to leave another friend in the lurch is quite likely to play the same trick on you.

When you've picked your friend and destination, the next tricky part is making up your mind on what to pack. More holidays have been ruined by bad packing than you'd care to imagine! You don't want to take too much, especially if you're backpacking. Even an hotel holiday can get off to a bad start if you sprain a wrist lugging 2 suitcases to and from the airport.

flip!

flop!

If you are going somewhere warm or with central heating, you can quickly wash a few clothes in a basin. Even if you are going to be at a disco each night, you won't need a new outfit each time. It's amazing how different a basic jeans-and-T shirt can look if you add new accessories each night. And, *nobody* looks at shoes, so you really only need one pair each for day and night. On a week's holiday, aim to have one change of clothing each for day and night, and enough jewellery, scarves, ties or belts to make up 5 different "looks". Add an extra set for a 2-week holiday. If you're heading for the beach, you'll need 2 costumes, or 3 if you want to look really flash! *They* don't take up much space. Hotels usually provide towels – check with the travel agent – but don't forget soap, shampoo, deodorant and toothpaste and brush. These can be very expensive if you are going abroad, and who wants to spend precious holiday time on this type of shopping? Girls may find it a good idea to take some tampons or sanitary towels. Even if your period isn't due, the excitement of going away may bring it on.

One item you might like to consider brings us to a very important subject. The item is birth control. The subject is holiday romances. Being on holiday can have a funny effect on the most steady person. When you are away from home, you feel free from all sorts of restraints. There are no parents, brothers or sisters, neighbours or teachers or bosses to tut-tut and tell you what to do. You may feel that you can do anything, and no-one will know. You can also feel that, just as the "holiday you" may remain behind when you go home, so will anything you do. Lots of people who at home would never dream of getting intimate after only knowing someone for a few days will do so on holiday. Partly, this can be due to the great feelings of relaxation. You have no worries and everyone is having a good time. Partly, it is because you think that no-one is going to tell you off. Partly, it can be because the atmosphere is so different that it seems romantic and made for love.

Sometimes you can be pushed into going further than you would like by your friends. If you go away with a group who seems to think the whole aim of the trip is to "score" as many male or female conquests as possible, you can come under fire if you don't join in. The problem is that half the time they are not doing as much as they say. Many a pregnancy has been started by boys and girls whose friends were only telling tall stories. If you've picked your friend well, you won't end up in this pickle. If you do, hold out for what you really want. You're not being a kill-joy – just refusing to be a sheep!

But if you think you would give in to such feelings, what should you do? Being on holiday will *not* protect you from the everyday realities of sex. Even wild, passionate sex under a Mediterranean moon can give you VD and lead to pregnancy! Do you really want to bring home a reminder of a holiday that might outlast your sun-tan? Both sexes would find a disease could harm them. And pregnancy is no joke, either. If you are a girl, it could lead to great unhappiness. If you are a boy, it could mean both a moral and a financial responsibility. You might think it clever to avoid this by using a false name or address. Very smart! And such a louse may not care that a girl, her friends and her family hate and despise him for his selfishness. Sticks and stones may break bones, but words . . . But it's funny how ratting on even a stranger can come back at you. Your friends may say they think you a "bit of a lad," . . . but "lads" are never trusted.

It makes sense, then, to pop some protection into your toilet bag, along with the sun-tan and insect bite cream. However squeaky-clean and gorgeous your holiday lover looks, he or she *could* be carrying a sexually transmitted disease. So, as well as pregnancy, you will want to be protected against this possibility. Probably the best choice is sheaths or condoms. If you use them properly, they will guard against both pregnancy and most types of VD. They also make a good point. If you are willing to use them, you show that you care about what happens to your new girlfriend. If a boy refuses, he tells you he couldn't care less how much pain a few minutes of his pleasure costs you. And if he sneers: "You're certainly experienced", you can jibe back: "And you certainly aren't!"

The best way to enjoy a holiday romance without regrets is to draw the line at kissing. In fact, if the romance is to be short-lived, holding hands, hugging and kissing can be more exciting if you *don't* take the next step to sex. It's a bit like spending a day working up an appetite for a super meal and being dished up grot. The anticipation tasted better than the real thing! If this really is a great love, you can do something about it at home when you've known each other a bit longer. If you aren't going to see him or her again, do you really want to go that far? Some of you might, and some may not. If you do, make sure a broken heart is not made worse by other problems.

It may seem stuffy, but make sure you protect your holiday in 3 other ways. Check you have insurance to cover any medical emergency. Check you have any necessary vaccinations for foreign travel – your travel agent or doctor will advise you on this. And, thirdly, take your holiday money in traveller's cheques if you are going abroad. Only change enough of these each day to get you through till next morning. This may be a bore and cost you a few pennies more. But it will cost you a lot more if you break a leg or get robbed and have not taken these sensible precautions.

If you take the trouble to think about your first holiday on your own *before* you go, you can relax at the time and really enjoy yourself.

27. Moving Out

'I didn't really think about leaving home until I was 17. Then, suddenly, I couldn't wait. All I thought about was having a place of my own, without being nagged and told when I had to be in' – Marie S.

At some time during your teenage years, you may well start thinking about leaving home. Perhaps you want more privacy. Perhaps you'd like more freedom. Perhaps you and your parents argue all the time. Getting a place of your own may seem the obvious answer. But is it? Leaving home is not quite as simple as it sounds. Before you pack your bags, it might be worthwhile thinking about a few things. Will moving out bring you freedom – or a lot of work? Can you look after yourself? Will you live alone or with friends? How will you find a new home? How will you furnish and run it? How much will it cost?

Moving out does seem such a good idea. Without Mum and Dad to nag you, you can come and go as you please. You can see your friends when you want and play music at all hours. You can eat what and when you choose, and nobody will complain about your clothes.

But hang on! Freedom brings with it responsibility. Sure, you can eat what and when you like, but *you'll* have to do the buying and cooking for each meal. You can't live on beefburgers and Chinese takeaways all your life. Not only would it be expensive – it would be very boring! You can dress as you please – but *you'll* have to do the laundry and cleaning. There are so many things you take for granted when living at home. You accept and expect good meals appearing on time. You reach for toothpaste and clean underwear and never think about how they got there! You may not think that cleaning and dusting is very important. An untidy room is one thing. A filthy home is another.

You might be surprised at how much time and effort is needed to keep yourself in a state *you* find pleasant. And how much it costs to buy everyday things you will find important, such as soap, deodorant, lavatory paper and toothpaste.

Playing music to all hours and having your friends round also seems great. Until you have to get up in the morning for college or work. You may then find that there was a reason for all that boring stuff about early nights!

Living on your own in a small flat or bed-sit may seem fun. But it can also be very lonely. You may find yourself spending longer in pubs or with people you don't really like to avoid going home on your own. So when you first leave home, it's probably best to go to a mixed home or hostel. First-year college students do best living in "Hall" or other university accommodation. This may seem to be going straight from one set of rules to another, but it will give you time to get used to looking after yourself. It will also give you a chance to meet people on other courses and widen your social circle. In your second year, you can then get a flat with friends.

Living with friends, or taking a room in a house or flat with new people, can be great. It can also be disastrous! Those nice friendly people you shared good times with can also have some pretty funny ideas about how to share living space. A bad living companion is happy to help themselves to your shampoo and cornflakes and in return give you their half of the washing-up! It may seem petty, but it's a good idea to sit down and work out who does what before you move in. It would also be a good idea to draw up a rota of duties. Everyone then takes it in turn to keep common areas clean. Some flatmates take it in turns to cook meals, and contribute to a "kitty" to buy food. If you never know when you'll be in, it might be better to have separate store cupboards with strict rules about replacing anything that is borrowed. You may think it's boring to have all these things agreed. Here you are trying to get away from rules! And doesn't it show a lack of trust? Maybe, but it's better to talk these things out *before* it all goes wrong and you have a quarrel. If you leave it until after, you may never be able to sort yourselves out. Rules are a bit like walls. They can be built to keep you in. They can also be there to protect you from the nasties outside!

Before you leave, work out how much money you will have, and how much you need. Whether you get your money from a student grant, your parents, a job or Social Security, your costs will be the same. You will need to pay out a certain amount each week or month for rent, and rates if these are separate. You will also have to pay for electricity and gas. These may be on a meter, which is expensive but means the bills do not build up behind your back. Getting a quarterly bill – one every 3 months – can be a shock. All the services – electricity, gas and telephone – will help you to avoid this. You can pay them a set sum every month. This is called a "Budget Account". You will also have to fork out for food, clothes and household goods. The best thing to do is to sit down with your Mum or Dad and work out with them how much they have to spend on these items. Obviously a family of four in a large house uses more than a single person in a bed-sit. However, be honest with yourself. You may not have to buy furniture polish, but you may also be the only person in the house getting through three jars of honey a week!

You might decide, having thought about all this, that family life isn't so bad after all! If you are earning money with a job or getting a grant as a student, you might try for a compromise. You could offer your parents a deal. You would like to stay at home but have more freedom. In exchange, you will contribute to the running of the house. If you pay your way in both money and a reasonable amount of work, it is quite fair for you to ask for more say in how you act. It is quite unfair, however, to be earning good money, taking all the advantages of home life and not doing a damned thing for it!

How much should you give? This will have to be something you work out between you. Remember, however, that you *will* leave home eventually, even if you wait until you get married and don't do that until your late 20s. So if you get into the habit of not paying your way at home and always having lots to spend on yourself, you could be in for quite a shock!

A good idea is this. Have your parents work out how much

they spend each week or month on all essential expenses. This means rent or mortgage and rates, fuel bills, food and household bills, fares and petrol. Work out what *proportion* this is of your parents' take-home money. You'll probably find it comes to about a half of the take-home pay. Then work out your own expenses – fares, lunches and clothes. Of the remaining sum, give your parents the same proportion as they have *left* after essential costs. So, if they have 40% of their money left after household bills, you give them 40% of your left-over money. If you're not earning much, you'll still have some left over to enjoy yourself. But it will mean that you will have a say in the house rules in the future. You should also take over a fair share of work if you are not doing chores already. Perhaps you could make a meal for everyone once a week – good practice for the future. By the way, *all* this applies to boys as well as girls. There's nothing clever and masculine in being unable to cook a meal, make a bed or do the laundry.

THIS APPLIES TO BOYS AS WELL AS GIRLS

The law is vague about when you can and cannot leave home. Teenagers are "minors", that is, children rather than adults until they are 18. Up to this age, your parents *must* look after and provide for you. So, until you are 18, you can't leave without your parents' permission. However, if your Dad or Mum threatens to throw you out, you should recognize they're pretty angry with you and make some effort to discuss matters. But, in law, they can't actually do it. In practice, if you did leave home, they would have to go to a lot of trouble to force you back. If you were under 17, they could have you put "in care": you would either be made to live at home or be put into a hostel or with foster parents. If you are a girl and ran away before you were 16, the people you stayed with could be in trouble for "harbouring" you and even be accused of "abducting" you. In other words, even if you went of your own free will, they could be accused of kidnapping you! If, as a girl, you were 16 or 17 and left to live with a boyfriend, because you would obviously be having sex, he can also be charged with the same offence. But the law *does* recognize that people over 14 can know their own minds and, if you had a good reason for wanting to leave home, your views *would* be taken into account.

Getting a home of your own can be difficult. You can look for:

1) Council housing
2) Private accommodation

Council houses and flats are in short supply. This means that in most cases you have to go onto a waiting list. You can ask to be put on such a list when you are 16. To do this, you contact your local Housing Department. This will be listed in the phone book under the Council's name. They will work out who comes high on the waiting list by using a points system. Someone who is homeless and has two children has more points than a single teenager still living at home. If you have anywhere to stay – even a friend's floor – you will *not* be considered to be homeless.

However, many councils have "hard to let" flats and houses. These are usually places they cannot offer to most people. It may be a large flat suitable for a family but at the top of a block with no lifts. Or a house with an outside loo. There may be no public transport nearby. These types of places can often be perfect for a group of young people willing to share, and to put up with a little bit of bother. They are usually offered "first come, first served", rather than by waiting list. Ask your local Housing Department how they offer such homes.

However grotty a council house may be, it would be given to you at a fair price and with fair conditions. You might have a better chance of getting private housing, but it can cost much more. Flats and houses to rent are usually advertised in local newspapers. Some estate agents also handle them, and there are special renting agencies in large cities. You can find these in your phone book or see their advertisements in your paper. An agency will charge you for finding you somewhere. Some ask a fee for going on their books. Some will ask you to pay the same as a week's or month's rent when they find you a place. Some ask both! If you end up paying *more* than a month's rent, that is a bit steep!

The Housing Department doesn't only deal with council homes. They, too, can advise you about hostels and may even know of flats and houses to rent privately. It's worth asking for their help.

When you find a place, you may be asked to pay two sums of money in addition to the first week's or month's rent. One sum may be called a "deposit", and this would be to cover any damage or loss of the owner's property during your stay. It is reasonable to be asked for this. However, you *must* insist on a receipt and a list of everything this sum covers. Make sure that any damage – such as marks on the walls or carpets – is written down, so that you cannot be blamed or charged later. If there is no damage or loss, you get the deposit money back when you leave.

The second amount you might be asked for won't be returned. Landlords used to ask for "key money". This was, frankly, a bribe! Flats are in such short supply that landlords can ask a lump sum just for you to be allowed to take over the place. Key money is now against the law, so some of them get round this by selling you "fixtures and fittings". In a good flat, this may cover carpets and curtains that then legally become yours. You could take them with you, or sell them when you move on. In a bad flat, "F and F" could mean one light bulb, and is just used as a means to get more money from you.

You are protected quite heavily by law. You can't be asked to leave without proper notice and, even then, you mustn't be thrown out. The landlord can't put up the rent unfairly. If you think he is charging too much, you can go to the Rent Tribunal and have a fair rent fixed. If the rent is fair but you don't have much money, you can go to the Housing Department and ask for help with rent and rates. The rent is the amount you pay to the landlord for the flat or house. "Rates" are the monies you pay to the Council. This covers street lighting, libraries, dustbin collection and all the other public services you use. In most private accommodation, the landlord pays the rates and builds this into your rent. If you take a flat or house, rates, electricity and other bills will probably be "exclusive" of the rent – or down to you to pay. If you join a group you may find that such bills are "inclusive" or included in your rent. So always check what is "inclusive" or "exclusive".

When you take a flat or a house, insist on having a Rent Book to keep a record of how much you pay, and when. If a landlord refuses to give you one or makes excuses, this is cause for concern and caution. The Rent Book is your protection. It proves how much you have to pay and that you have paid it. Without a Rent Book, the landlord can give you notice to quit unfairly and claim you have cheated him. If you take him to the Rent Tribunal, he can lie about how much you are charged. The problem is that he has the upper hand. He'd have no trouble finding a new tenant, but you might have difficulty finding a new flat. You'll have to decide which is the more unpleasant choice – stay or go.

Most rented flats come with furniture, crockery and some bedding. You can get the rest by various means. Your parents might let you take sheets and even some furniture. They'd probably let you have some pots and pans. Buying new things can be expensive and it is not a good idea to get into debt by buying on hire purchase or "HP" at this stage. You'd be surprised how cheap and good second-hand goods can be. Look in the "For Sale" columns of your local paper. Search through the cards people put up in local newsagents. Go to charity shops such as Oxfam and Age Concern. You may find household goods sold at local auctions – these sales would also be advertised in your local paper. You can get a whole stack of china or cutlery for 50p if you're lucky. And don't forget jumble sales; they can be a gold mine!

Leaving home is a big step. However awful home life may be, try not to jump off into the big wide world in a hurry. Running away from home will never solve your problems. You're likely to take those with you. But if you think the time has come for you to branch out, then do it. If your parents are unhappy at their little boy or girl leaving, the best way to show them you can manage is to plan carefully and keep everything under control.

A Last Word

Nothing ever stands still – that is one of the most important lessons in life. People, relationships and circumstances grow and change – and sometimes end and die. The most successful and happy adults are not those who seem to have everything battened down and under control, but those who are relaxed enough to "go with the flow". Human beings have been bumbling through, making mistakes and being more or less happy for centuries, so just because you have a few problems and can't seem to solve them, don't despair. You won't be unusual! Just remember: bumps and bruises were a natural part of your learning to walk as a very small child. So, moments of pain, embarrassment and confusion are a part of learning to stand on your own two feet as a fledgling adult. To end up as a truly mature human being, able to manage on your own, you *have* to make your own mistakes. No-one can do your growing up for you. If you can recognize that you're not aiming for perfection, but to be able to get by and if you can keep your eyes, ears and mind open . . . then the chances are, whatever is thrown at you during your teenage years, you'll survive.

Good luck!

Help! Some Useful Addresses

We all need help at some time in our lives. If you have a problem, why not ask:

your parents

a friendly and sympathetic teacher

a youth club leader

or a local priest (you don't have to be a church-goer)?

There are also lots of groups ready and willing to give you a
hand with *any* problem. Some will have a local office near you.

Look up the following in your own local telephone book:

COMMUNITY HEALTH COUNCIL – if you have a complaint about
the medical profession or need any advice about your health.

FAMILY PRACTITIONER COMMITTEE – if you want to change your
doctor and are having trouble doing so, or have a serious complaint against your GP.

SEXUALLY TRANSMITTED DISEASE or "SPECIAL" CLINIC – most
hospitals have one. They'll see you without a letter from your
doctor and will keep your visit private if you insist. Usually listed in the 'phone book under "VD".

SOCIAL WORK DEPARTMENTS – if you have family problems and
would like to talk to a social worker, look in the 'phone book
under the name of *your* Council or under "Social Services Department".

SAMARITANS – if you feel really down, find their number in the
'phone book or just ask the operator to put you through.

The groups listed on the following pages often have London
addresses. If you live elsewhere, this *doesn't* mean that there is no
help in your area. Contact the main address and they will be
able to put you in touch with *your* nearest help.

Help with sex

Brook Advisory Centres
153A East Street
London SE17 2SD
01-708 1234
These are birth control clinics especially for young people. They can also offer help with pregnancy and relationship problems.

Family Planning Association
27-35 Mortimer Street
London W1N 7RJ
01-636 7866
Can send you leaflets and books on a wide range of sexual subjects, and will have the address of your nearest birth control or youth advisory clinic.

British Pregnancy Advisory Service
Austy Manor
Wootton Wawen
Solihull
West Midlands B95 6BX
05642 3225
If you are pregnant and don't know what to do, or want an abortion and your own doctor or birth control clinic won't help you, this private charity will.

Life
7 Parade
Leamington Spa
Warwickshire
0926 21587
If you are pregnant and *do* want to keep the baby, they can help.

One Parent Families
255 Kentish Town Road
London NW5 2LX
01-267 1361
Can give lots of advice on how to manage if you are left holding the baby.

Gay Youth Movement
BM GYM
London WC1N 3XX
If you think you are gay and want to talk to other young people in the same boat.

London Gay Switchboard
01-837 7324 (24-hour service)
or write to them:
BM Switchboard London WC1N 3XX
If you are gay and need someone to talk to.

Lesbian Line
01-251 6911
or write to them: BM Box 1514
London WC1N 3XX
If you want to talk to other women about being gay.

Parents Enquiry
16 Honley Road
London SE6 2HZ
01-698 1815
Can help you and your parents come to terms with someone in the family being gay.

Incest Crisis Line
66 Marriot Close
Bedfont
Middlesex
01-422 5100 or 01-890 4732
If you or anyone you know is suffering sexual advances from a member of or a close friend of the family.

Incest Survivors Campaign
Hungerford House
Victoria Embankment
London WC2N 6NN
01-836 6081
Offer the same help, but to women only.

London Rape Crisis Centre
PO Box 69
London WC1X 9NJ
01-837 1600 (24-hour service) or 01-278 3956 (office hours)
If you've been sexually attacked, they can offer sympathy, advice and practical help.

Help with the law
Childrens Legal Centre
20 Compton Terrace
London N1 2UN
01-359 6251
Will help you if you feel anyone – including parents and tea-chers – is not giving you a say in what is happening to you, just because you are young.

Citizens Rights Office
1 Macklin Street
London WC2
Will advise you on your rights.

National Council for Civil Liberties
21 Tabard Street
London SE1 4LA
01-403 3888
Can advise you if you feel an injustice is being done to you or anyone you know.

Equal Opportunities Commission
Overseas House
Quay Street
Manchester M3 3HN
061-833 9244
Can support and help you if you are refused the right to do any-thing – join a club, do a school course, have a job – just because of your sex.

Citizens' Advice Bureaux
115-123 Pentonville Road
London N1 9LZ
01-833 2181
Can help and advise on any subject. They have local centres.

Help with holidays and leaving home
National Trust
36 Queen Anne's Gate
London SW1
   or
British Trust for Conservation Volunteers
36 St Mary's Street
Wallingford
Oxfordshire OX10 0EU
0491 39766
Both run holiday 'work camps' to preserve the countryside and old houses, and need volunteers.

Voluntary Service Overseas
9 Belgrave Square
London SW1X 8PW
01-235 5191
Train and send volunteers to the Third World for periods of a year or so.

Concordia YSV Ltd
8 Brunswick Place
Hove
East Sussex BN3 1ET
Organize working holidays on overseas farms.

Shelter
157 Waterloo Road
London SE1 8XX
01-633 9377
If you've left home and can't find a place to live, they will try to help.

Help with something to do
National Association of Youth Clubs
Keswick House
30 Peacock Lane
Leicester LE1 5NY
0533 29514
Can tell you about youth clubs in your area.

Penfriends Worldwide
60 Ellesmere Road
Benwell
Newcastle-upon-Tyne NE4 8TS
0632 736732
Can put you in touch with a penfriend anywhere in the world.

Youth Hostels Association
Trevelyan House
St Albans
Herts AL1 2DX
Will give members a complete list of all their hostels – very
cheap and good accommodation when you are on holiday.

Sports Council (England)
16 Upper Woburn Place
London WC1H 0QP
01-388 1277
   or
Scottish Sports Council
1 St Colme Street
Edinburgh EH3 6AA
031-225 8411
Will be able to tell you about sports available in your area.

Help with your money and being a customer

The Office of Fair Trading
Field House
Bream's Buildings
London EC4 1PR
01-242 2858
If a shop is giving you a bad deal, they will help.

Association of British Launderers and Dry Cleaners
Lancaster Gate House
319 Pinner Road
Harrow
Middlesex HA1 4HX
01-863 7755
If a dry cleaners has lost or damaged something of yours, and is refusing to pay up, complain to the Association.

Association of British Travel Agents
55-57 Newman Street
London W1P 4AH
01-637 2444
If you are going on holiday, make sure your travel agent is a member of this. If anything goes wrong, they will see you are given a fair deal.

National Consumer Council
18 Queen Anne's Gate
London SW1H 9AA
01-222 9501
Will help you with any complaint against a shop or manu-facturer.

Help with your health

Anorexic Aid
The Priory Centre
11 Priory Road
High Wycombe
Bucks
0494 21431

Anorexic Family Aid Information Centre
Sackville Place
44 Magdalene Street
Norwich NR3 1JE
0603 621414
For help if you or anyone you know has eating problems or is
dieting too much.

Overeaters Anonymous
PO Box 539
London W11 2EL
01-584 3157
If you or a friend just can't stop 'binge' eating.

Health Education Council
78 New Oxford Street
London WC1A 1AH
01-637 1881
or
Scottish Health Education Group
Health Education Centre
Woodburn House
Canaan Lane
Edinburgh EH10 4SG
031-447 8044
Have excellent leaflets and books on how to become, and keep,
fit and healthy.

National Eczema Society
Tavistock House North
Tavistock Square
London WC1H 9SR
01-388 4097
If your teenage acne is *really* bad, they can advise you.

Patients' Association
Room 33
18 Charing Cross Road
London WC2H 0HR
01-240 0671
If you have any problems with the way the NHS has treated you.

Medic-Alert Foundation
11-13 Clifton Terrace
London N4 3JP
01-263 8957
If you have any medical problem that could make you collapse, such as diabetes or an allergy to penicillin, they can make you a bracelet or medallion that would tell a doctor what was wrong.

Royal Association for Disability and Rehabilitation
25 Mortimer Street
London W1N 8AB
01-637 5400
If you, a friend or member of your family has a handicap, the Association can help and advise you.

Mind
22 Harley Street
London W1N 2ED
01-637 0741
Can advise and support you if anyone in your family has a mental illness or problem.

Help with parents and family

Women's Aid Foundation
374 Grays Inn Road
London WC1X 8BB
01-837 9316
If you or your mother is being battered at home, Women's Aid
could offer a local shelter where you could stay and be safe.

National Society for the Prevention of Cruelty to Children
67 Saffron Hill
London EC1N 8RS
01-242 1626
If you or someone you know is being treated cruelly, the local
NSPCC workers will help.

Stepfamily
Maris House
Trumpington
Cambridge CB2 2LB
0223 841306
Advice and support for stepchildren and their parents.

National Marriage Guidance Council
Herbert Gray College
Little Church Street
Rugby
Warwickshire CV21 3AP
0788 73241
Sympathetic help for *any* relationship or sexual problem for you
or your parents.

National Association of Young People's Counselling and Advisory Services
17-23 Albion Street
Leicester LE1 6GD
0533 554775
Can give you addresses of someone near you who could help
with a problem.

CRUSE
Cruse House
126 Sheen Road
Richmond
Surrey TW9 1UR
01-940 4818/9047
If there's a death among your family or friends, they can help you with sympathy and advice.

Help with your education and career

Open University
Walton Hall
Milton Keynes MK7 6AA
If you missed out on university, you could catch up by doing an Open University degree in your own time, at home. You don't need exam qualifications to be accepted on a course.

Advisory Centre for Education
18 Victoria Park Square
London EC2
Information and advice on school and college courses.

Higher Education Information Centre
Middlesex Polytechnic
Queensway
Enfield
Middlesex
Information and advice on what college courses and grants are available.

Your local Job Centre and Careers Office (listed in your 'phone book) will give you up-to-date information and lots of help on choosing school and college courses to suit you, and on local training schemes and work experience.

Help with ill-health and drugs
Alcoholics Anonymous
PO Box 514
11 Redcliffe Gardens
London SW10 9BQ
01-352 9779
If you have a drinking problem, they can help you overcome it.

Al-Anon Family Groups
61 Great Dover Street
London SE1 4YF
01-403 0888
If someone in your family is an alcoholic, they can help you cope.

Release
1 Elgin Avenue
London W9 3PR
01-289 1123
01-603 8654 (emergency)
Can help and advise with any drug-related problem.

Families Anonymous
88 Caledonian Road
London N1 9DN
01-278 8805
Can help you and your family if one of you is a drug taker.

ASH
5-11 Mortimer Street
London W1N 7RH
01-637 9843
Will give help and advice to stop smoking.

TRANX
17 Peel Road
Wealdstone
Harrow
Middlesex HA3 7QX
01-427 2065
Can support you or a member of your family in coming off
tranquillisers.

Index